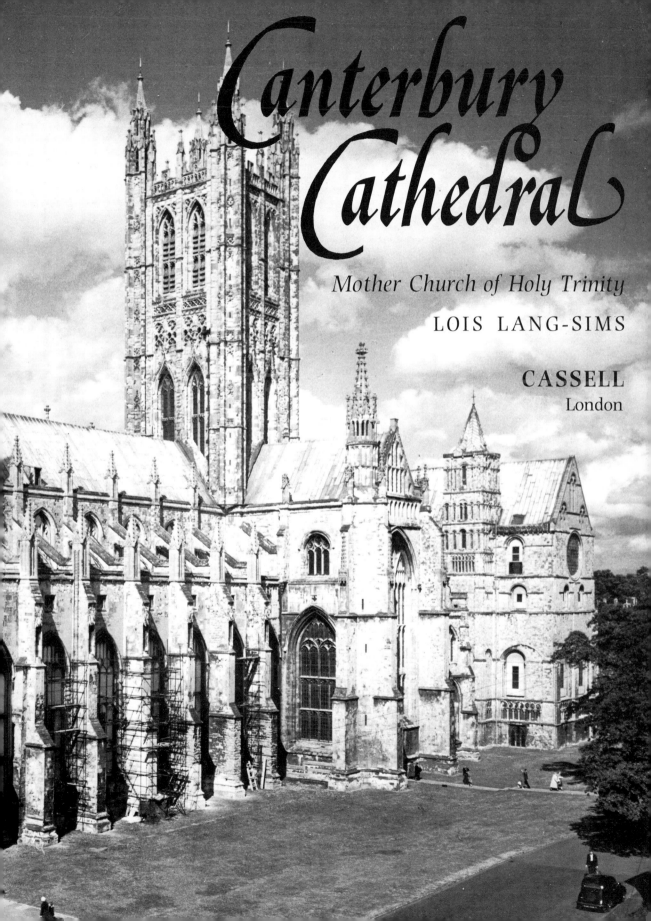

Canterbury Cathedral

Mother Church of Holy Trinity

LOIS LANG-SIMS

CASSELL
London

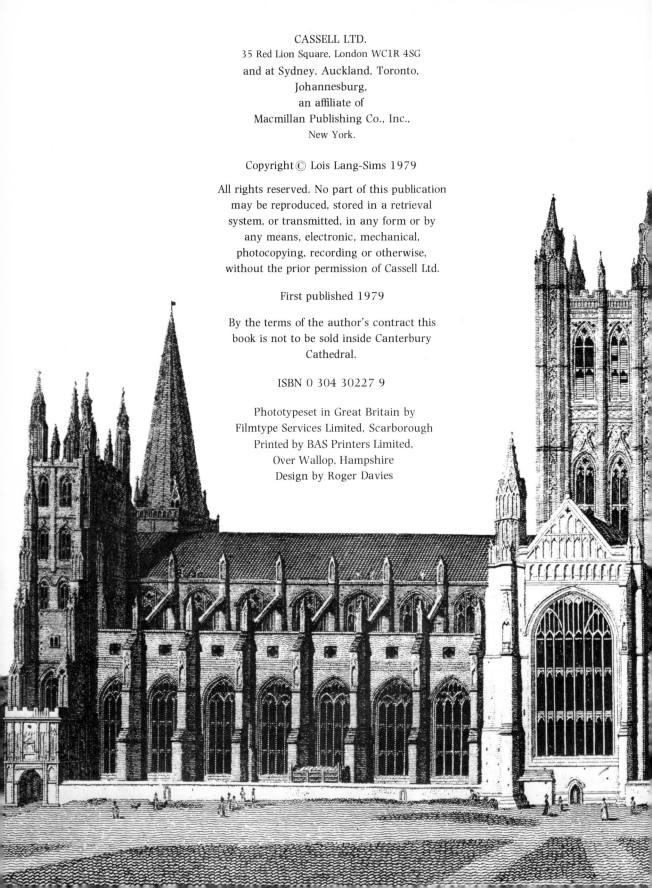

CASSELL LTD.
35 Red Lion Square, London WC1R 4SG
and at Sydney, Auckland, Toronto,
Johannesburg,
an affiliate of
Macmillan Publishing Co., Inc.,
New York.

First published 1979

By the terms of the author's contract this
book is not to be sold inside Canterbury
Cathedral.

ISBN 0 304 30227 9

Phototypeset in Great Britain by
Filmtype Services Limited, Scarborough
Printed by BAS Printers Limited,
Over Wallop, Hampshire
Design by Roger Davies

To Nowell, Kezia and Keren
in memory of
Hewlett Johnson
DEAN OF CANTERBURY

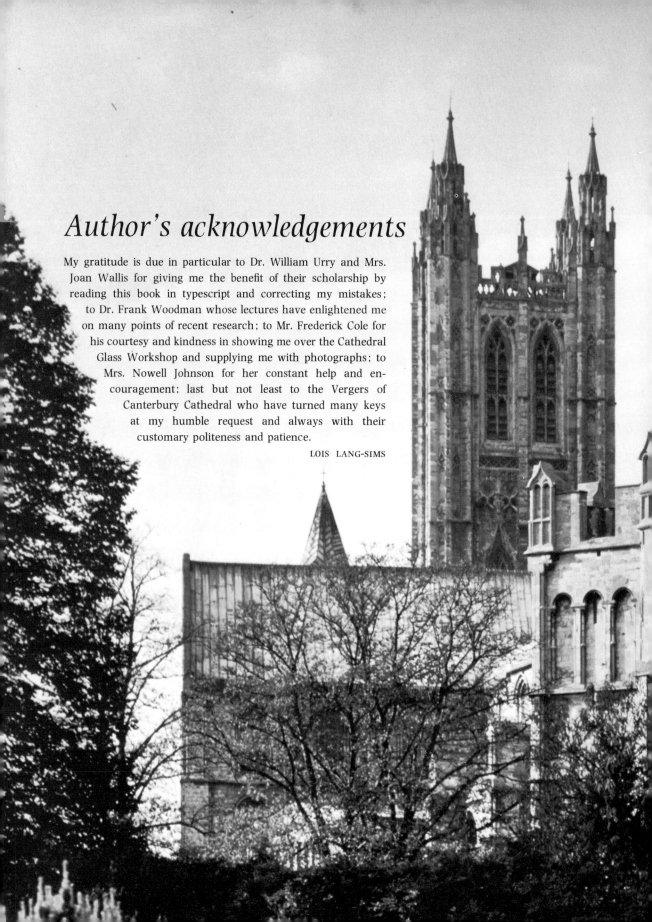

Author's acknowledgements

My gratitude is due in particular to Dr. William Urry and Mrs. Joan Wallis for giving me the benefit of their scholarship by reading this book in typescript and correcting my mistakes; to Dr. Frank Woodman whose lectures have enlightened me on many points of recent research; to Mr. Frederick Cole for his courtesy and kindness in showing me over the Cathedral Glass Workshop and supplying me with photographs; to Mrs. Nowell Johnson for her constant help and encouragement; last but not least to the Vergers of Canterbury Cathedral who have turned many keys at my humble request and always with their customary politeness and patience.

LOIS LANG-SIMS

For now have I chosen and sanctified this House,
that my Name may be there for ever:
and mine Eyes and mine Heart
shall be there perpetually.

2 Chronicles, 7. 16.

Table of events

This table should be consulted in conjunction with the lists of Archbishops, Priors and Deans on pgs 160–1.

597	Arrival in Canterbury of Augustine and his monks. Baptism of King Ethelbert. Augustine builds his Cathedral on the site of an old Roman-Christian church.
758	Death of Abp. Cuthbert, the first Abp. to be buried in the Cathedral.
942	Repairs to the Cathedral under Abp. Odo.
1011	Abp. Alphege taken prisoner by the Danes.
1012	Abp. Alphege murdered.
1023	The body of Abp. Alphege restored to the Cathedral in the presence of King Canute.
1067	Saxon Cathedral burned to the ground.
1070	Abp. Lanfranc begins to rebuild the Cathedral. Rebuilding completed in 7 years.
1096–1107	The eastern end of Lanfranc's Cathedral is pulled down and a new Quire and Crypt built under the auspices of Prior Ernulf.
1108–1126	Under the auspices of Prior Conrad the new Quire is finished and decorated.
circa 1160	Prior Wibert's water system. Water Tower built. Many other important building operations, probably including a great Cloister.
1164–1170	Exile of Abp. Thomas Becket.
1170	Murder of Abp. Thomas Becket.
1174	Penance of King Henry II. Burning down of 'Conrad's glorious Quire'.
1175	William of Sens begins rebuilding the Quire.
1178	William of Sens falls from the scaffolding and is incapacitated.
1179	William the Englishman replaces William of Sens. Visit of King Louis VII. Presentation of the Regale.
1180	Dedication of the new Quire.
1207–1213	Exile of the monks as a result of a quarrel with King John.
1220	Translation of the body of St. Thomas to the Shrine in the Trinity Chapel.

circa **1300**	Prior Eastry's screens installed in Quire.
1376	Funeral of the Black Prince.
1391—1405	Nave rebuilt (Yevele and Stephen Lote).
1420—1428	St. Michael's Chapel built out of SW transept.
1424—1434	SW tower rebuilt (Thomas Mapilton).
1437	Tomb of Henry IV and Queen Joan.
1439	Holland tomb completed.
1448—1468	Rebuilding of 'Martyrdom' transept, with 'Deans' ' chapel.
1496	Beginning of final stage in the building of Bell Harry Tower (John Wastell).
1513	Visit of Erasmus and Colet.
circa **1517**	Completion of Christ Church Gate.
1528	Elizabeth Barton in Canterbury.
1538	Destruction of the Shrine of St. Thomas.
1540	Dissolution of the monastery.
1541	New governing body of the Cathedral instituted by Royal Charter.
1564	Huguenot services commence in Crypt.
1571	Death of Odet de Coligny.
1573	Visit of Queen Elizabeth.
1625	King Charles I and Queen Henrietta Maria at the Cathedral. Death of Orlando Gibbons.
1642	Puritan soldiers wreck the Cathedral.
1643	Unseemly activities of 'Blue Dick'.
1660	Visit of King Charles II.
1662	Order in Council confirming the privilege of Huguenots to worship in the Crypt.
circa **1670**	Beginning of 'change' ringing in England.
1787	Repaving of the Nave.
circa **1800**	Demolition of the turrets on Christ Church Gate.
1832	Rebuilding of NW tower.
1935	Completion of the restoration of Christ Church Gate. 'Murder in the Cathedral' (T. S. Eliot) performed in Chapter House.
1936	'Cranmer of Canterbury' (Charles Williams) performed in Chapter House.
1939	Air raid precautions in Cathedral. Removal of the glass.
1940	Alfred Deller becomes a lay-clerk. Bombing of the Deanery and other houses in the Precincts.
1942	(June 1st) Severe raid centred on the Cathedral. (June 24th) Spontaneous service of dedication in the Nave.
1946	(July) Thanksgiving Service in the presence of King George VI, Queen Elizabeth and Princess Elizabeth.
1958	Death of Miss Margaret Babington.
1961	Enthronement of 100th Archbishop (Dr Michael Ramsey).

Key to plan of Canterbury Cathedral

1 SW Porch. 15th century.
2 SW Tower (Dunstan). 15th century.
3 West Door. Beneath the Great West Window, containing the Adam.
4 NW Tower. Arundel. 19th century. Copy of SW Tower.
5 Nave. Last decade of 14th century. Perpendicular.
6 Font. 17th century.
7 Nave altar.
8 Screen of the Six Kings. Early 15th century.
9 NW (Martyrdom) Transept. Mixed: Early Norman (Lanfranc) and 15th century.
10 Becket's Doorway.
11 Tomb of Archbishop Peckham. Beneath the Royal Window of Edward IV.
12 Chapel of Our Lady (Deans' Chapel). Late 15th century.
13 Norman Doorway to Western (Ernulf's) Crypt. Early 12th century.
14 SW Transept. 15th century.
15 St. Michael's Chapel and Holland Tomb. 15th century.
16 Tomb of Archbishop Stephen Langton.
17 Whall window. 19th century.
18 South Door. Beneath the Window of the Patriarchs.
19 North Quire aisle. Mixed: Norman, Transitional. Bible windows.
20 South Quire aisle. Mixed: Norman, Transitional. Tomb of Prior Henry de Eastry.
21 Quire. Late 12th century. Transitional. William of Sens.
22 High Altar.
23 NE Transept. Mixed: Norman, Transitional. With Chapels of St. Martin and St. Stephen.
24 Memorial to Archbishop Tait. Late Victorian.
25 Passage to upper storey of Water Tower.
26 Tomb of Archbishop Chichele.
27 Norman Tower (N). Mid 12th century.
28 SE Transept. Mixed: Norman, Transitional. With Chapels of St. John and St. Gregory.
29 Norman Tower (S). Mid 12th century.
30 Chapel of St. Andrew. Early 12th century. Norman.
31 Treasury. Mid 12th century.
32 Chapel of St. Anselm. Early 12th century. Norman. With 14th century (Decorated) Window.
33 Trinity Chapel (site of Shrine of St. Thomas). Late 12th century. Transitional. William the Englishman.
34 Tomb of the Black Prince.
35 Tomb of Archbishop Hubert Walter.
36 Tomb of Odet de Coligny.
37 Corona. With Patriarchal Chair.
38 Tomb of Henry IV.
39 Chantry Chapel of Henry IV. 15th century.
40 Tomb of Dean Nicholas Wotton. 16th century.
41 Cloisters. Late 14th century (much restored).
42 Passageway with piers (early 12th century) from Monastic Dormitory.
43 Modern Library on site of Monastic Dormitory.
44 Chapter House. Mixed: 14th, 15th century with Victorian glass.
45 Water Tower. Mid 12th century (upper storey 15th century).
46 Entrance to 'Dark Entry' (East walk of Infirmary Cloisters), leading to Green Court.

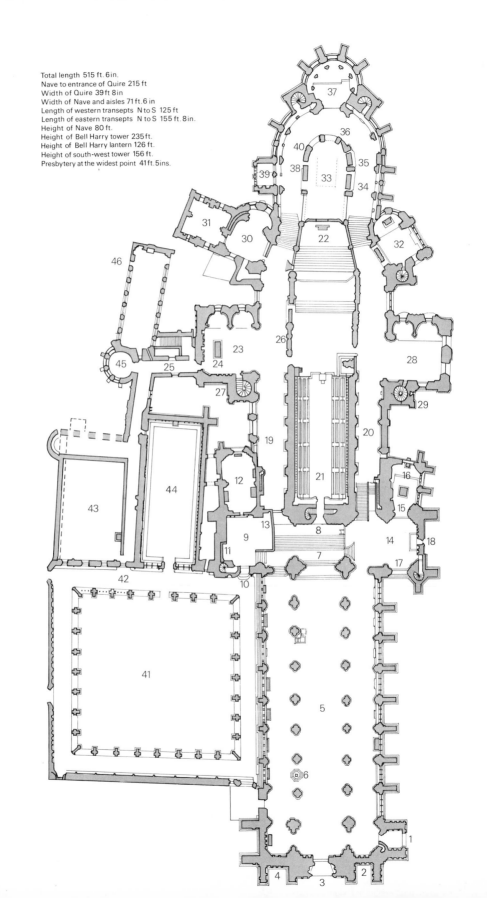

Total length 515 ft. 6 in.
Nave to entrance of Quire 215 ft
Width of Quire 39 ft 8 in
Width of Nave and aisles 71 ft. 6 in
Length of western transepts N to S 125 ft
Length of eastern transepts N to S 155 ft. 8 in.
Height of Nave 80 ft.
Height of Bell Harry tower 235 ft.
Height of Bell Harry lantern 126 ft.
Height of south-west tower 156 ft.
Presbytery at the widest point 41 ft. 5 ins.

O<small>N JUNE</small> 24th 1942 an unpremeditated service was held in the Nave of Canterbury Cathedral, called by the Mayor and conducted by the Archbishop. To this service came flocking so many of the citizens that even Canterbury's Nave could scarcely hold them; and that was a time when the population of the city was depleted beyond the imagination of its present teeming inhabitants. Three weeks earlier, on the night of Trinity Sunday, 'the holy mother church of Holy Trinity' (as Archbishop Thomas Becket was in the habit of calling it) had been the target of an air attack lasting from one o'clock in the morning until three. Continuous dive-bombing had reduced the Precincts to a shambles, and the whole of that area of the city to what seemed to the emerging shelterers, when the attackers were gone, to be a roaring furnace. Not one of those shelterers had expected to find the Cathedral still there – untouched. And yet it was. In the city itself there was tragedy and loss of life; but the Church of the Holy Trinity stood undamaged, ringed about with fire, and no one within its Precincts had been hurt.

In wartime it is easy to believe in the miraculous. Certainly there was one, at least partial, explanation of this particular 'miracle', in the shape of the Fire Service and ARP personnel who, for two hours, had been sprinting up and down ladders all over the roof, picking up the fire-bombs as they fell, and chucking them down on to the grass. The fact, however, remains that during the Second World War fifteen high explosive bombs fell in the Precincts, and the Cathedral itself was not hit. In the highly charged atmosphere of that time, many people believed that its saints had been protecting it. Others said simply that it was a storehouse of power. No doubt it was all a coincidence. But what is coincidence? a coincidence of what?

In any case, on that 24th of June, the citizens of Canterbury went to their Cathedral to give thanks. They thanked God 'that this holy and beautiful house of prayer' had not been damaged by the bombs. Also for the 'courage, steadfastness and friendliness' which had been evoked when 'all so readily worked together to save life, to check damage, and to lighten the burden of those who suffered'. They prayed for the bereaved and commended to God those who had lost their lives. The Cathedral was decked with summer flowers: roses, peonies, delphiniums, irises, white foxgloves and Canterbury bells.

After the war a 'Service of Thanksgiving' was held in the presence of King George VI and Queen Elizabeth. There have been royal occasions, many of them of the utmost splendour, in Canterbury Cathedral since the days of King Ethelbert. Monarchs, beloved and not so beloved, have been welcomed there: Canute brought the gift

Opposite
A view taken from the Archbishop's Canterbury home. Above the Cloisters, from left to right: NE transept; Norman tower; Chapter House; NW (Martyrdom) transept; Bell Harry Tower; East end of Nave.

of his crown; Henry II came barefoot to kneel at the tomb of St. Thomas and submit to the most humiliating chastisement; King Stephen and King John were crowned in the Cathedral; the Black Prince came to it with his prisoner the King of France; Elizabeth the First rode on horseback to the West door; Charles the Second, returning from exile, came straight to Canterbury from Dover and paused there to attend a service. No visiting King or Queen deserved or received a greater welcome than was given by the citizens of Canterbury, in the summer of 1946, to the man who had been their wartime monarch. But those who remembered that earlier service in the midst of the war, inevitably thought of it as an infinitely more moving experience.

This holy and beautiful house of prayer: was it perhaps Archbishop William Temple who thought of those words to describe the Cathedral – or was it Dean Hewlett Johnson – or Precentor Joseph Poole, that lover of economy and accuracy in words – or Mayor Lefevre, descendent of the Huguenot refugees who were granted in perpetuity a place of worship in the Crypt, by one of the greatest gestures of ecumenism in the history of the Church?[1]

The Cathedral is holy and it is beautiful. Beauty and holiness do not always go together; but where they do not there is a lack, in so far as the innermost reality is not outwardly expressed. Beauty is order; it is that which Simone Weil has called 'the Order of the World'. It has to do with the Second Person of the Trinity, the Creative Word which issues in those 'fair forms' which will lead us, according to Plato, to the knowledge of Truth. In the Christian tradition Man is potentially the perfected Image of the Divine: therefore the Cathedrals and churches of Christendom were designed in the form of a Man, which is also the form of a Cross. These things have to be realised before we draw near to such a place; they have to be realised actually to enable us to draw near to it – with more than our mere feet.

[1] Since writing the above, I have realised that the words must have been taken from Archbishop Cosmo Lang's moving paean of praise to the Cathedral, on the occasion of his resignation in March 1942, which began: 'Of all the sorrows of parting, I think the saddest is parting from this holy and beautiful House of God.'

NOTHING EXISTS apart from its context. If the Cathedral bestows a peculiar character upon the city which it dominates, equally its own character is determined by the city and by the Kentish countryside: the Cathedral is what it is by virtue of its precise position on this globe; it has affinities with the particular quality of the atmosphere and the light in one particular place. The Cathedral belongs to

Canterbury and to Kent.

Throughout its recorded history Kent has been, on the whole, a fruitful well-ordered locality, producing a type of men and women remarkable for their staunch stability and pride. The Romans, in no uncertain manner, left their mark upon it. In Canterbury, or Durovernum as they called it, they established a prosperous city with an enormous theatre and at least one temple which appears to have been the centre of an important cult. A considerable deposit of votive coins near the site of this temple, together with the bones of animals ritually sacrificed, suggest that Canterbury was a place of pilgrimage in the second and third centuries after Christ. But the Romans were late arrivals in these parts. The Celts were here first; and there is a strong tradition, supported by archeological evidence, of Druidic influence. Possibly a connection exists between the original character of the city as a centre of religious life, and the fact that it afterwards became the Lourdes of medieval Europe. In any case it has, and has always had, a double image: that of the temple and the shop. Canterbury has been, and proudly so, a city of shop-keepers and merchants, their feet planted firmly on this earth. John Boyle, in his *Portrait of Canterbury*, observes that the city has a claim to be known as the Mother of the Bank of England; since its mint (which was flourishing in the first quarter of the seventh century) had the distinction of striking the first penny, as an act of homage to Offa, King of Mercia, by the Kings of Kent.

Formerly a vital junction of Roman roads, the city retained its importance as lying on the direct route to London from the coast of France. In its medieval heyday the place was a teeming hive, in which the majority of the citizens did well for themselves and had an eye to the main chance in this world as well as the next. The poor they had always with them; but even the poor had a fine selection of Religious Houses at the doors of which they might supplicate for the leavings of the monks: Blackfriars and Greyfriars, to say nothing of the two great rival establishments of St. Augustine's Abbey and the Cathedral Priory of Christ Church. A quarrelsome lot they all were. The pilgrims, of course, must have got on their nerves; in exactly the same way as the tourists streaming over to Canterbury from the continent get on the nerves of indigenous Canterburians in the present. The citizens had a good deal to put up with from other directions as well. If the pilgrims were frequently troublesome, so were the monks. Kings and Archbishops, confronted by the Prior's representatives in truculent mood, had been known to shut themselves up in their palaces and refuse to come out. Not untypical of the relations between the sacred and the secular in Canterbury was the action of one enraged citizen who smote one of the brethren smartly over the head 'with a halybut' – which sounds as if it might have been a formidable medieval weapon, until we learn that the aggressor was a fishmonger and the two protagonists were haggling over the price of fish.

It is an odd thought that anyone returning to Canterbury now, after an absence of thirty years, would experience more difficulty in finding his way about than if he were suddenly to be transported eight hundred years into the past. By the twelfth century the city was well and solidly laid out. Burgate was by then an old-established street. It must have been, in part at least, this quality of solidity and permanence, triumphing over bloodshed, fire and epidemic, which gradually bestowed upon Canterbury its overweening civic pride: a pride of clanging bells and pullulating life: a pride, later on, of self-complacency and intellectual sleep, as the sound of bells became dreamier, the ecclesiastics sleeker, the poor less indiscreetly evident, the ivy thicker over Prior Sellenges Gate. In the nineteenth century *Ecclesia Anglicana* must have dominated the city as surely as ever it was dominated by the monks. Slipping to and fro in its streets went the black figures, tightly encased: Canons, Archdeacons, Bishops: black aprons, black gaiters, black cockaded hats. Supreme in his own Cathedral was the Dean. The Archbishop himself could only preach in the Cathedral by permission of the Dean who, more than anyone else, was an individual of unique but entirely local and specialised importance. Those were 'the soft quiet seasons' as Eliot put it in *Murder in the Cathedral*. Dickens, in *David Copperfield*, writing of the ragged little boy (more real to us now than any of those clerical ghosts) who stole through the streets of the city on his way to seek shelter with his aunt, evokes that Victorian scene and sets it delightfully within its context of the fields of Kent.

> I seemed to be sustained and led on by my fanciful picture of my mother in her youth, before I came into the world. It always kept me company. It was there, among the hops, when I lay down to sleep; it was with me on my waking in the morning; it went before me all day. I have associated it, ever since, with the sunny street of Canterbury, dozing as it were in the hot light; and with the sight of its old houses and gateways, and the stately grey cathedral, with the rooks sailing round the towers.

Opposite
The Virgin and Child Enthroned. East Window of the Eastern Crypt. About 1190–1200.

Canterbury is strongly associated with this particular book. It contains the house which Dickens imagined as belonging to Mr. Wickfield, where David spent his youth in the company of Agnes. Those of us who have had a lifelong devotion to this novel are still

arrested occasionally, in the midst of all the noise and agitation which nowadays obliterates the cawing of those rooks, by a mental picture of David and Agnes, hand in hand, walking primly together through Christ Church Gate on their way to Sunday morning church.

Christ Church Gate: entrance to the Precincts.

Opposite
Part of one of the early thirteenth century 'Miracle Windows' in the Trinity Chapel. The upper row of panels illustrates the story of Robert of Rochester, a naughty little boy who threw stones at frogs and was saved from drowning by St. Thomas.

Christ Church Gateway is the way to the Cathedral for the vast majority of those who visit it. (The alternative approach, by way of the Mint Yard and the Green Court, is chiefly for the Kings School and those of the Cathedral staff, including the Dean, who live on the north side as did the Prior and his monks.) Despite the band of shield-bearing angels which forms the principal decoration of the Gate, it is a thoroughly secular-looking edifice. Begun but not finished during the priorate of Thomas Goldston II, it displays in a prominent position his punning rebus of three gold stones. Above them are the mitre and staff, generally the prerogative of Bishops, but granted to the Priors of Christ Church as a mark of favour by the Pope.

Prior Goldston II died in 1517, shortly before the completion of

Christ Church Gate: detail of Archbishop Juxon's wooden doorway restored in the reign of Charles II. The upper panel bears the arms of the Dean and Chapter.

[1] The date 1507 inscribed upon the gate when it was restored in the 1930's is now believed to be erroneous.

[2] *Memorials of Canterbury Cathedral.* Woodruff & Danks. Chapman & Hall Ltd. 1912. Hereafter referred to as W. & D.

his Gate,[1] leaving a sum of money for the finishing of it. Three years later, in the Spring of 1520, not so many years before the dissolution of the monastery and the plunder of the Shrine of St. Thomas by King Henry VIII, that same monarch rode jauntily beneath the new and gleaming Gateway in the company of the Emperor Charles V. The two young men were greeted by Archbishop Warham and by Prior Thomas Goldwell, after which they paid their respects at the Shrine and proceeded to the archiepiscopal palace, there to be entertained at 'incredible expense'. Prior Goldwell, who was destined to be the last of his line (his rebus of a gold well is also to be seen on the Gate) must have been thankful that, on this occasion at least, the privilege of playing host had not fallen upon himself.

The Gateway is smothered in heraldry, most of which has to do with the royal family and the Church. Directly above the main archway is the coat of arms of King Henry VII: Lions passant guardant in pale or and lilies or, with a greyhound and a red dragon as 'supporters' of the shield. Elsewhere we can pick out the Rose-en-soleil crowned, the badge of the combined houses of Lancaster and York; and the Beaufort portcullis, reminder of the castle where the ubiquitous Beauforts were sired by 'old John of Gaunt'. Comparing the present appearance of the Gate with the old prints and etchings depicting it in the eighteenth century, one would suppose that its main structure had undergone no startling changes between that period and our own. Great is our surprise therefore, in coming upon prints and photographs belonging to the years between 1800 and the mid-thirties of this century, to find that its charming octagonal turrets have unaccountably vanished. The tale of the twin turrets, as by chance it has been preserved in a letter written by one Prebendary George Gilbert, takes away one's breath.

'My father', writes the Reverend gentleman, 'was one day in the bank of Simmons and Gipps at the corner of St. Margaret Street; Alderman Simmons and Jesse White (then cathedral surveyor) were present. The exact time of day was asked by the Alderman, who said, "If those turrets of the cathedral gate were away we should see the church clock from the bank door. Can't you pull them down, Jesse?" "It shall be done", replied Jesse; and it was done.'

This same Jesse White ('a man of substance', says Mr. Gilbert, 'in body and in pocket') adorned the Nave with wooden pinnacles and was responsible for various other curiosities in the same material, so that Canon Danks in his invaluable *Memorials*[2] observes that if he (Jesse White) had lived to the age of Methusala — which seems to be a charitable way of saying that if he had not died when, thank

God, he actually did — 'it is conceivable that our descendents would have had a wooden Cathedral'. In any case, they were left with a flat-topped Gate; until, under the auspices of a later Cathedral architect (W. D. Caroë) and with funds donated by the Friends of Canterbury Cathedral, the entire structure was carefully cleaned and meticulously restored — and the turrets were popped on again as neatly as if they had never come off.

This work was completed in the mid-thirties, at about the same time that *Murder in the Cathedral* was commissioned for the Friends Festival and performed in the Chapter House. The Friends, in those early days of their existence, had their office inside the Gate. Amid so many activities, the Steward and Treasurer was in her element, her vintage bike propped up against the wall, her typewriter clacking on into the silence of the night, long after the heavy wooden doors, bearing Archbishop Juxon's Arms, were shut and locked. Not Archbishop Becket himself was more of a figure in his day than Miss Margaret Babington in hers, straight as a rod and thin as a stick, with her carrotty hair and her nose like a precision instrument and her flowered silks, perched up high on her bike — that startling old machine that was a kind of local personality in itself. Certainly she was the most remarkable individual ever to inhabit Christ Church Gate.

Christ Church Gate has the disadvantage, however, of leading directly to something which distracts the attention immediately and entirely away from it. Even the present day tourists, although they appear to be, for the most part, too preoccupied with taking photographs actually to look at the Cathedral when they first see it, dive beneath the Gateway and, positioning themselves against it, tilt their cameras upwards and sideways at the view beyond.

As one passes through the Gateway and enters the south-west corner of the Precincts, the impact of the Cathedral produces a particular kind of shock, sudden and overwhelming without being in any way violent. The eye is carried upwards in a stroking movement. It rises to the height of Bell Harry tower, and comes back to the lesser height of the twin towers, Arundel and Dunstan, with an effect upon the psychosomatic system similar to that of the ancient plainsong music of the Church.

One does not in fact perceive the whole length of the building from

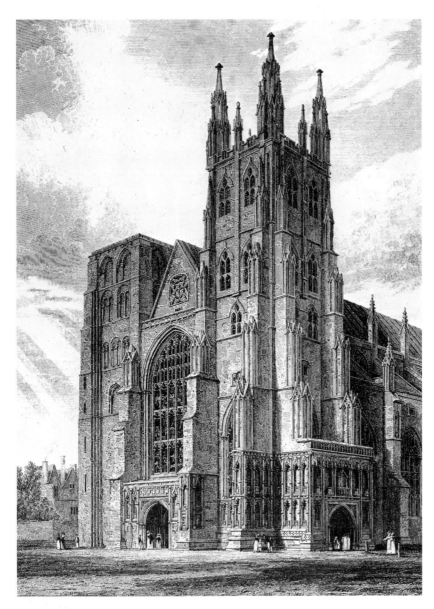

this standpoint. The presbytery and the Trinity Chapel are obscured by the jutting out of the south-east transept; and yet one is not misled: the proportions are so nearly perfect that what is not seen is unconsciously understood. If people would only have the patience to stand quietly for a time in this corner of the Precincts, simply looking at the Cathedral before going into it, they would find themselves being lifted into the dimension to which it properly belongs; so that when they are ready to go in their minds will be open to its influence.

Gothic architecture has the peculiar characteristic of combining

in an ideal balance the qualities of etheriality and weight. In this way it is an expression in stone of the teachings of the Church. Each one of the great religions has its own particular emphasis. Christianity has laid stress upon the mysterious paradox of the descent of a Divine Being into the depths of earth, so that matter itself may be spiritualised and raised up. A building such as Canterbury Cathedral, designed and erected in accordance with principles evolved and handed down through generations of craftsmen within the context of the Christian faith, demonstrates the possibility of combining the utmost possible impression of earthy weight with the utmost possible impression of weightless aspiration to the apex of the celestial vault. This is achieved by means of the geometrical proportions of the building as a whole, together with the soaring nature of its various features with their intricate and delicate ornamentation, every feature having a practical function to perform, every function being enlisted in the service of a meaning beyond itself.

The exterior of the Nave is visible in its entirety from Christ Church Gate. This part of the Cathedral was built in the late fourteenth and early fifteenth centuries on the site of the old norman Nave of Archbishop Lanfranc; hence it is later in style than the Quire, which lies to the east. This is the style known as Perpendicular, a term covering English Gothic architecture during the period *circa* 1335–1530. Bell Harry tower, which was actually erected during the last decade of the fifteenth century, is conservative in style, harmonising so unerringly with the Nave as to seem as if both were the work of a single architect; although, in fact, almost a century elapsed between the two great building operations which they represent. Bell Harry was raised under the auspices of John Wastell, the architect responsible for Kings College Chapel in Cambridge. Wastell may have been basing his work upon earlier plans, a considerable gap having occurred between the first putting in hand of the project and its final carrying out. Prior Sellenge, in a letter to Archbishop Morton, which must have been written very shortly before his death, refers to the matter as follows:

Most Reverent father in God, and my most singler gode Lorde, after all due recommendation and humble obediens promysed, please it the same to understande that Master Surveyour and I have communed with Jo. Wastell your mason, berer hereof to perceyve of hym what forme and shappe he wylle kepe in resyng of the pynacles of your new towre here. He drew unto us 2 patrons of hem: the one was with doble fineall withowt crocketts and the other was with crocketts and sengle fineall. Thys 2 patrons please it your gode Grace to commaund the seyd Jo Wastell to draw and shew them unto you and upon the syth of them your Grace

Symbols of the Evangelists against the sky at the eastern end of the Cathedral. *Left* The eagle of St. John.

shew hym your advise and plesure whyche of them 2 or of any other to be devised shal contente your gode Lordeshyp to be appoynted. And further-more if your gode Grace wolde require the seyd Jo Wastell so to do, I thinke that he myth so provide that this pynacles may be finished and accomplyshed this nex somer folowyng. The whyche if it myth so be than your towre outward shuld appere a werke perfite.[1]

[1] From a MS in the archives of the Dean and Chapter.

It did so appear. It is the glory of Canterbury Cathedral, inferior in beauty to nothing which the hand of man has ever devised to the glory of God.

T<small>O-DAY THERE</small> are five towers: Bell Harry; the twin towers of Arundel and Dunstan at the west end; and another pair of twins, the smaller, norman towers, built for staircases rather than bells, which fit into the angles between the main building and the eastern tran-septs. A puzzle is connected with these two. The one to the south, which we see as we approach the Cathedral, is frequently referred to as St. Anselm's tower, although its date, controversial as this may be, has never been given as less than twenty years after Anselm's death. The twelfth century plan of the monastic waterworks (*circa* 1164) by the monk Eadwine, depicts the twin chapels of St. Andrew and St. Anselm, further east, as being ornamented with similar towers, which have since vanished. On the other hand, there is no sign in his plan of the towers attached to the eastern transepts. For the purpose of attacking this puzzle, we should recall that Augustine's Cathedral was burned down in the latter part of the eleventh century and rebuilt under the auspices of Archbishop Lanfranc. Some thirty years later, during the priorate of Ernulf, the Quire of this relatively new building was pulled down and re-erected on a much larger scale; only to be destroyed in a second conflagration in the year 1174. From this point onwards, for the next two hundred years, the Cathedral consisted of Lanfranc's Nave and the Quire and Trinity chapel as these were rebuilt after 1174, together with those portions of Ernulf's building which had escaped being burned — including the two chapels, from which the towers had by this time been removed. Were the towers destroyed while their chapels re-mained intact? or, as Mr. Colin Dudley would have us believe, were they transferred bodily by the new architect, William of Sens, to the position which (according to his theory) they now occupy in the angles of the east transepts? Mr. Dudley's theory would explain Eadwine's drawing and also the persistent association of the south-

Right The Winged Lion of St. Mark. Date uncertain: probably 18th century.

east tower with the name of St. Anselm. On the other hand, the drawing could equally be explained by the fact that Eadwine was not so much concerned to depict the Cathedral as to illustrate the water-works: one has only to study his plan to realise that the south-east transept tower would have got in the way of one of his pipes.[1]

The Cathedral is rich in such conundrums. They are part of its character, which is that of a building which has grown over centuries of time, binding together different periods and their corresponding styles in a perfectly satisfying but always intriguing coherence. It was not until the Victorian era that ecclesiastical authorities and architects began to think in terms of actually copying the past. The nineteenth century was an age of almost frenzied restoration, with a peculiar passion for what was known as the 'middle-pointed' style, a sort of neo-fourteenth century cook-up. To make way for these creations, norman building was quite frequently pulled down, while Jacobean woodwork was carelessly thrown out as so much scrap. There was, however, in the midst of all this, one great and – the dust having cleared, we are nowadays inclined to admit – predominantly sobering influence: that of Sir Gilbert Scott. Sir Gilbert left his mark upon almost every one of our English cathedrals. In Canterbury, successive architects (notably George Austin who rebuilt the north-west tower, and W. D. Caroë whose name has already been mentioned in connection with the Gate) were, in general, obedient to his principles, which were those of exact fidelity to the original rather than hectic attempts to out-gothic the Gothic. The wooden pinnacles of Jesse White (themselves, of course, replacements) were taken down and replaced by others in stone, which harmonise so well that one does not notice them as being substitutes for the original fifteenth century work.

Nowadays, of course, there is general recognition of the value of new work in a contemporary style. Present day restorers combine this with a proper respect for the past, assisted by a variety of new techniques; so that when the stonework of a building such as Canterbury Cathedral has to be replaced, this is done not only with the loving fidelity recommended by Scott, but with the kind of expertise that was not at the disposal of nineteenth century architects.[2] It is seldom realised by those who gaze up at the Cathedral from Christ Church Gate, how much of what they are seeing is not the original stone with which it was built. The stone used by Lanfranc, and later by successive builders from the eleventh century to the nineteenth, came principally from the quarries near Caen. Lanfranc had been Abbot of the monastery at Caen, which may

---

[1] Another, more recent, theory suggests that the transept towers were actually the work of Prior Wibert, undertaken after Eadwine's plan was completed. It has further been suggested that the towers of St. Andrew and St. Anselm were much larger, covering the entire area of the chapels they surmounted.

[2] These remarks represent an ideal. Constant vigilance is required on the part of the general public to ensure that this ideal is invariably carried out.

'The Cathedral is rich in such conundrums': the SE (Norman) tower associated with the name of Anselm.

have been one reason for his choice; but the principal reason was economic. Canterbury was two miles only from the port of Fordwich on the Stour. It was a great deal cheaper to ship the stone across the channel from Normandy to Sandwich, convey it from there to Fordwich on barges and then by wagon to the site, than it would have been to drag it many miles along atrocious roads from an English source. That Caen stone was aesthetically suitable does not require pointing out. It had the additional advantage of being easy to work.

Unfortunately it is relatively porous, and disintegrates in a damp climate more quickly than some of the stone which has been used since. Nowadays the Cathedral is being restored with Lepine stone, also from France, a beautiful and durable material which, although it may appear rather startlingly white to us at present, is expected to weather in due course almost exactly to the colour of the original stone: in contrast to the various other materials which bestow upon Bell Harry tower its pleasantly mottled appearance. Doulting stone, an orangy stone from Rutland, the yellow bathstone so unfortunately popular with the Victorians, are only some of the varieties of material which appear on the face of the building, whether we notice them or not. Like a human being, although less frequently and thoroughly, the Cathedral changes its skin from time to time. Unless we are romantically desirous of having a ruin on our hands, we cannot expect anything else.

The north-west or Arundel tower is a startling example of fidelity to the ideals of Sir Gilbert Scott. Old prints, showing the western towers before the 1830's reveal them as having been not only asymmetrical but separated by 350 years, the one being a remnant from Lanfranc, while the other belongs to the early fifteenth century when the whole of the Nave and its transepts were rebuilt. Some time in the 1820's it was noticed that the old norman tower was showing signs of collapse. A certain Thomas Hopper, a London architect, was requested to examine it and make a report. His conclusions were that the foundations, together with the inner ashlar and pillars, were sound; and the whole could be restored and made safe. 'Under all circumstances', he wrote, 'the surveyors do not recommend the taking down of the tower, which, notwithstanding its defects, is an interesting relic of the most ancient style of ecclesiastical architecture.' However, take it down they did. George Austin, the surveyor and architect to the Dean and Chapter, took upon himself the task of designing and having built an exact replica of the south-west tower; with the result that the Cathedral's west front has presented a symmetrical appearance ever since. The Caen stone of this new tower weathered so badly that in less than a century the outer skin had to be almost entirely replaced (the Cathedral gasworks which were situated for some time, unaesthetically, at its foot can hardly have done it any good). At the core of the construction the old norman ashlar work remains intact. Lovers of the Cathedral differ fiercely on the question of its north-west tower. Many agree with Mr. Hopper; although one assumes that even these purists, when they contemplate the Cathedral in the only way which enables one fully to appreciate the arrangement of its three principal towers – that is to say from a distance – are not displeased with what they see. In any case there was no doubt of the approval of Sir Gilbert Scott.

T HE NORTH-WEST tower was named the Arundel tower after Archbishop Arundel who, in the fifteenth century, presented the Cathedral with four bells which were known as the 'Arundel ring'. These bells were originally in the central tower; they were moved to the north-west or Arundel tower when the former was rebuilt. Their names, bestowed in a solemn ceremony of blessing on April 8, 1409, were St. Blaise, St. Gabriel, St. Mary and St. John the Evangelist. The names of bell towers are frequently those of their bells. The south-west tower is known as St. Dunstan, after a bell of that name commemorating the saintly archbishop. The skills of that versatile craftsman included that of bell founding; however, the original Bell Dunstan itself was cast in the fifteenth century in the days of Prior Molash. Bell Harry is the namesake of Prior Henry de Eastry, the Grand Old Man of Canterbury, who ruled over the monastery for more than forty years and died in 1331, with a long list of building works to his credit, the outcome of his combined administrative and imaginative gifts. Presumably he was actually the donor of the bell *Henricus*, referred to for the first time in the year 1288. This would have been hung in the old norman tower, known as the 'Angel Steeple' on account of the great gilded Angel which surmounted it and was visible for miles around; thus Bell Harry tower itself is considerably younger than its bell. Nearly two hundred years after the death of Prior Henry, his bell *Henricus* appears in a sacrist's account which is worthy of the unbowdlerised Pepys: *item cum eodem pro i Clapir de belle hary 2s. 6d.*

There is a 'ring' of twelve bells at Canterbury at the present time. These are situated in the south-west tower; and to ring all the changes on them would take thirty-eight years. Standing in the south-west corner of the Precincts on a sunny morning when the bells are clanging in celebration of some great feast day of the Church, one can fall under a kind of spell, when it seems as if the building itself were joyously crying out. Only the change-ringing which is peculiar to the English tradition has the power to produce this spell. On the continent the Church rings 'carillons', which are beautiful in their own way; but it is an altogether different way.

Even in England the practice of ringing the bells in a mathematical sequence goes back no further than 1668. Erasmus, when he visited Canterbury and described its towers as 'filling the air far and wide with the clang of brazen bells', was certainly not referring to it.

St. Dunstan is also the clock tower. The chimes of the Canterbury clock are based upon the eighth Gregorian tone and have the power to induce serenity of mind, although nowadays it is difficult to hear them properly except at night. That charming and lovable clergyman, the Reverend Francis Kilvert, heard a story at first hand on the subject of this clock. In his diary for June 27th 1876[1] he tells us that he 'went to Canterbury on pilgrimage, nine miles, but by train' from Faversham, and went to Evensong at the Cathedral in the afternoon.

As I waited in the stalls for the service to begin one of the vergers told me the sad recent story of the poor man who was burnt to death by the ignition of some benzoline oil with which he was cleaning the clock. 'He had to creep into a hole like the mouth of a large cannon', said the verger, 'and another man held a candle behind to light him. But this was against orders. It was against orders to take up any light at all. Suddenly the benzoline exploded and shot the man out of the hole, blackened, stunned and blinded, like a cannon ball out of a gun. I saw both the men come tumbling down the ladder together hardly knowing what they were doing or where they were going. The man who had been blown out of the hole had his clothes all burnt off him and was entirely naked except his boots. I got a fly to the cathedral door for him. He looked around to see if any women were coming and then rushed into the fly and was driven to the hospital. But he could not rest night or day. All his skin came off. It took several men to hold him down in his agony and he died raving mad.'

'Twice or three times,' adds the diarist, 'Canterbury Cathedral has been in danger of being burnt down.' This was, already, an understatement. The Danes set fire to it until the monks were driven out by the molten lead dripping down on their heads from the roof. In 1067 the Saxon Cathedral was accidently burnt to the ground. Almost a hundred years later the Quire was gutted and had to be entirely rebuilt. Only a few years before the tragedy recounted by Kilvert, a terrifying conflagration had broken out in the roof of the Trinity Chapel, to be checked by the belated arrival of the Volunteer Fire Brigade and eighty troops from the barracks. (It was put on record at the time that for some hours after this fire had been put out, the interior of the Cathedral presented a magically beautiful appearance, filled from end to end with a mist of blue wood smoke. One can imagine it; and the picture must be easier to appreciate in

Opposite
Approach to the Cathedral from Christ Church Gate, showing the south west porch. The pigeons, which roost in the interstices of the building, have always been a part of the scene.

[1] *Kilvert's Diary.* Ed. William Plomer. Vol. 3. Jonathan Cape.

imagination than it was on the spot.) Kilvert goes on to describe the measures that were being taken to protect the Cathedral in future emergencies of a similar sort:

When I left the Cathedral after evensong all the good folks of Canterbury seemed to be in the Cathedral close and there was great excitement. The authorities had just got down a new steam fire engine for the protection of the Cathedral from the periodical fires which threaten it, and they were throwing a jet of water over the Cathedral roof, the water seething, foaming, boiling and bubbling in the great tub round the hose as the steam from the engine rushed and roared through it. A good deal of the water fell back from the north-western tower in spray, in which the bright sunshine made a brilliant dazzling wavering sparkling rainbow arch about six feet high.

As the jet of water was playing over the Cathedral roof I watched the jackdaws disturbed from their usually quiet haunts and sailing round and round the central tower at a great height in the cloudless sky, and I marked their shadows upon the grey rich sunny Tower, how they crossed and recrossed, shrunk and grew, disappeared and appeared again, flitting softly and silently to and fro like the dim ghosts of birds who had inhabited that tower centuries before.

Watchers in the Precincts, seventy years later, became familiar with the spectacle of jackdaws 'sailing round and round the central tower' because they had been disturbed from their haunts. Whenever a bomb fell upon Canterbury they behaved in this manner; however, on the night of the June raid in 1942, they must have prudently flown away altogether; for there was nothing sailing round the central tower that night except sparks. Sparks, like giant fireflies, performed a measured dance on the wind from the flames. They dipped and rose and curtsied in the air, drawing before the Cathedral a moving veil of jewelled openwork. The stones had turned blood red. Only those who live near the Cathedral can realise how subtly its walls reflect the light, changing their colour with every variation brought about by the weather and the passage of the sun. That night they were crimson-dyed against a pall of smoke. One of those watchers in the Precincts, coming out on to the glass-strewn steps of her home, only a stone's throw away from the south-west porch, forgot for the moment the danger that was past, even the possibility that some of her friends had lost their lives in the fire. In an autobiography published thirty years later, she wrote:

'Never before had I seen, never again would I see it so beautiful as this.'

FOR AN older generation at least, there is something automatically depressing about the story of St. Augustine, because we were taught it as children under some such heading as *How the Church came to England*; and most of us thought that 'going to church' was bad enough in any case without having to learn lessons about it. St. Augustine, we were told, was a 'missionary', a word which had horrible associations with missionary boxes and jumble sales – and more 'church'. We wished that St. Augustine had stayed at home. But had we been led to picture him as he must actually have been, a wild brave man inflamed with a passion for Christ, limping into Canterbury with his forty monks, chanting the praises of God, behind the swaying crucifix which was new to the wondering people who came hesitantly out to look – not just a 'crucifix' to them but a strange image of a tortured man splayed out – had we been able to picture him like this, we should have listened more eagerly perhaps. Nowadays there are better stories about him no doubt; but just as little understanding of the point.

Augustine came all the way to Canterbury from Rome, in the year of Our Lord 597, to preach the Word of Christ to King Ethelbert and his Court. The King of Kent, although he was himself presumably a follower of the 'old religion' (a mixture, one assumes, of the nordic mythology of Valhalla and Druidic lore), had a Christian wife. Queen Bertha was the daughter of the Frankish King. She had come over to England accompanied by her chaplain, Bishop Luidhard, with whom and with her attendant ladies, she was accustomed to worshipping in the little church of St. Martin outside the walls, a building left over from the days when the Romans were settled in Kent and Roman Christianity had flourished. But St. Martins was not the only relic of that vanished faith. Not far from King Ethelbert's palace there was a building which appears to have been the remains of another Christian church. Bede describes it as having 'been built in ancient times by the hands of Roman believers'. Augustine, he tells us, restored it with the help of the King 'and there he established an habitation for himself and for all his successors'. This was after the conversion of King Ethelbert, which seems to have been brought about easily enough, and was followed by the even easier 'conversion' of his subjects. Augustine consecrated his Cathedral 'in the name of the Saviour, our God and Lord Jesus Christ'. It is still known as Christ Church; although it has been associated particularly with the Holy Trinity and was popularly known by this dedication for some ten centuries from the time of its foundation by its first Archbishop.

The extent of the actual rebuilding that was necessary is not known. However, the finished appearance of the Saxon Cathedral may be reconstructed from a description written in the twelfth century by Eadmer, a monk of Canterbury, who tells us that it was basilican in form, having an apse at either end and two flanking towers or transepts. Beneath the presbytery, to the east, there was a lofty crypt. There were four important altars in the main body of the church. One of these was the altar of the Virgin Mary on the chord of the western apse, behind which was the *cathedra* or archiepiscopal throne, set at the extreme west end of the church in exactly the opposite place from that which it occupies at present.

The meaning of the word 'cathedral' derives from the seat or *cathedra* of the bishop. Whether or not Augustine originally pictured himself as the unchallenged head of the Church in England, he rapidly discovered that his primacy was a matter of dispute. There was, in fact, already an indigenous Church in Britain, although its influence had not extended to the south-east. Its origins are obscure; but it seems to have derived from the twin sources of Ireland and Gaul, and so to have been in essence a Celtic Church. It is told of Augustine that he journeyed to Wales for a parley with these native bishops and monks. They sought the advice of an old hermit, who counselled them to make sure that the new arrival was a man of God by testing his humility and forbearance. So they deliberately kept him waiting in a field, to see if he would rise to greet them courteously, without any sign of having been put out. Augustine, for some reason, did not rise; and so this first experiment in dialogue was not a success. A hundred years later, the seventh Archbishop of Canterbury, the great Theodore of Tarsus, succeeded in binding together in some sort of unity the scattered Church; but it was nearly four hundred years after that, in the time of Lanfranc, that the primacy of Canterbury over every other see in England was finally established, signed and sealed.

Opposite
An angel swirls about the central figure of Christ in glory in St. Gabriel's chapel.

Aᴜɢᴜsᴛɪɴᴇ ᴇsᴛᴀʙʟɪsʜᴇᴅ a monastic community in association with his Cathedral. Until it became a Benedictine Priory in the time of Lanfranc, this Community was known simply as the Christ Church convent. Throughout the Saxon era it was ruled by Deans; and there seems to have been a certain vagueness about its Rule and status. Augustine himself, when he came to die, chose to be buried in the Abbey which he had founded at about the same time, and

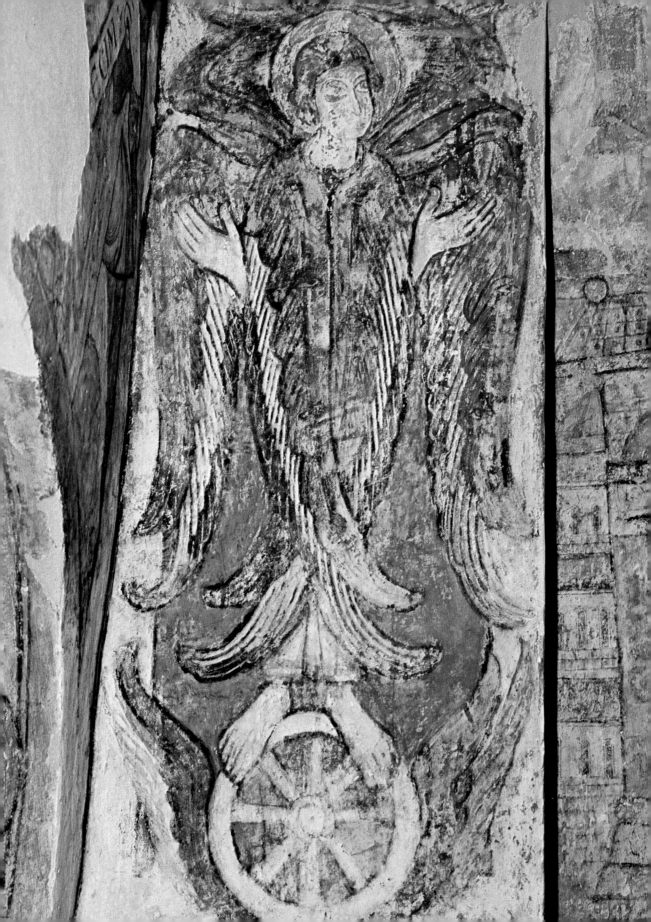

where for some years before his death he had practised the life of prayer as a simple Benedictine monk. This great Abbey of St. Peter and St. Paul, afterwards known as St. Augustine's – of which today we see little more than a prospect of rubble and the twin towers, greatly restored, of its principal Gate – was for centuries the powerful rival of the Convent (later the Priory) of Christ Church. The two establishments glared at one another across the city wall; and although the successive Archbishops of Canterbury were the titular Abbots of the convent, it was a point of burning resentment on the part of their spiritual sons that their bodies did not rest within its Precincts – but over the way, in the custody of the odious brethren of St. Augustine's, whose conceit knew no bounds as a result. This situation was peculiarly intolerable in that so many of these Saxon Archbishops were officially declared to be Saints. St. Augustine, St. Laurentius, St. Mellitus, St. Justus, St. Honorius, St. Deusdedit, St. Theodore of Tarsus, St. Tatwin (what was the matter with poor Berchtwald who appears between the latter two in solitary dis-eminence?): for a hundred and fifty years more or less, St. August-ine's collected them all; while the brethren of Christ Church grated their teeth.

The extraordinary passion for the acquisition of the corpses, bodily parts and personal belongings of the saints, which swelled to fantastic proportions in the early middle ages and powerfully influenced the history of the Church, is something we have got to understand before we can even begin to understand the Cathedral in the medieval heyday of its burgeoning life. We can appreciate its beauty from the start; we can study it as an historical monument; we can even say our prayers in it: but to picture what went on be-tween its walls and *why* it went on, and the living dynamics of the place, we must comprehend the cult of St. Thomas and the lesser cults which preceded it and the inner meaning of those cults, which relates to the inner meaning of Christianity itself. Why was it that lesser men battled over the bodies of the spiritually great, actually tearing them in pieces in order to become the proud possessors of an arm, a finger or a tooth?

Christianity has always been in danger of sliding into materialism. Of all the great world religions, it is the one which has most con-sistently stressed the holiness of the physical body and of the whole earth as a living sacrament. The Resurrection of the Body is one of the central doctrines of the Church. At the very core of its worship is a piece of bread and a cup of wine, not as symbols merely but as claiming a mysterious identification with the Christ. This emphasis

Opposite
The terrible seraph of the Book of Revelations: twelfth century wall painting from St. Gabriel's Chapel.

upon the physical extends, as it were, into every nook and cranny of the Christian faith. Behind the veneration paid to relics lies the idea of the potential holiness of the physical world actualised in the bodies of those men and women who have made of themselves pure vessels for the grace of God. Not, of course, that there is anything exclusively Christian in the cult: it exists in all times and places, even to the teenager who cherishes a scrap of material torn from a pop-idol's shirt. At the present time we are just beginning to approach such matters from a scientific standpoint. Controlled experiments, notably in the U.S.S.R., have established the objective reality of a blessing or a curse, of the capacity of inanimate objects to be endowed with psychical contents and – strangest of all perhaps – of the sympathy existing between an organism and its various parts, widely separated as these may come to be in time and space. We have to remember all this before we dismiss the people of the middle ages as preposterously 'superstitious'.

As the year 1170 solemnly closed on a Cathedral desecrated by the murder of its Archbishop, it must have been a sobering thought for the Christ Church monks that, had it not been for the admirable foresight of one of his predecessors in office, the body of St. Thomas would even at that moment be in danger of being whisked across the road by the rival establishment. Archbishop Cuthbert was the eleventh Archbishop of Canterbury, and the first to be buried within the precincts of the Cathedral church. He cherished an affection for the convent, which led him into devious machinations, as related by one William Thorne, a monk of St. Augustine's, who, in the fourteenth century, composed a Chronicle of the history of his House:

In the year 743 Archbishop Cuthbert grieved over the destitute condition of the Church over which he ruled, for it had no great men interred within its walls, inasmuch as when an Archbishop died the body was carried to the Monastery for burial according to the decrees of the Popes. Therefore conceiving sorrow and bringing forth ungodliness, he in his wickedness carefully thought out a plan for the changing of this custom; and repairing to Eadbert, who was then King of the land, with tears streaming down his face, he with the subtlety of the serpent, laid his case before the Dove-like and harmless King, earnestly imploring him to alter the aforesaid custom of burial and to confirm the alteration by his own Royal Command. With much difficulty, and more by the aid of money than by the power of his prayers, he at length gained his desire. Thus it came to pass in the year of Our Lord 758 the aforesaid Archbishop Cuthbert, being attacked with heart disease, and feeling that he was about to die, realised that the time had now arrived when the trick that he had planned might at length be played off against the Church of St. Augustine, and that the serpentlike birth which had been so long in the womb might now at last be produced, even though the birth pangs brought death in their train; he was lying by himself in his own Church as the end drew near, and summoning his whole household and the monks — who were nothing loth to obey — he bound them by a solemn oath not to divulge his illness nor his death, nor to give any signal thereof by the ringing of bells, nor to perform any funeral services for him, until he should have been buried several days. . . .

So it was that the Abbot of St. Augustine's had a lost journey; and a positively monumental loss of face. When the bell at last began to toll, he arrived, as was his wont on these melancholy occasions, at the head of a solemn procession of chanting monks, the processional crucifix swaying aloft — and there was no body there to be picked up. Over a gap of twelve hundred years one can almost see the smile on the face of the Dean as he bowed to the Abbot, suggesting perhaps that he should stay for a little refreshment. St. Augustine's, however, showed some spirit. When the next Archbishop (St. Breogwine) passed to his rest, Abbot Jaenbert proceeded to the Cathedral with an armed band and became so exceedingly militant that the brethren of Christ Church, much alarmed, elected him as their new Archbishop on the spot. After that St. Augustine's gave up.

Between the death of Archbishop Cuthbert and the burning down of the Saxon Cathedral in the year 1067, there lived and died two of the greatest Archbishops in the history of the English Church. On either side of the high altar their bodies were to lie, their gold, bejewelled shrines only a little less magnificent than that of St. Thomas himself: St. Dunstan and St. Alphege: the gentle craftsman and mystic, who died on his regulation bed of ashes on the ground, surrounded by his loving monks; and the martyr-saint who died, like Thomas, in a pool of his own blood.

Dunstan, who had been a monk of Glastonbury, was one of those extraordinary individuals who seem to be endowed with every imaginable gift. A great statesman and administrator, he was also a learned theologian, a skilled metalworker, an accomplished musician, a bell founder and an illuminator of manuscripts. With all this he was a man of prayer, around whom innumerable legends grew up to illustrate his sanctity of life. These ranged from the picturesque tale of his seizing the Devil by the nose with a pair of tongs, to the rather more credible story of the snow-white dove which fluttered down from the roof of the Cathedral and settled on his shoulder during the ceremony of his enthronement. This was in the year 960. His primacy lasted for twenty-nine years; and never can there have been an Archbishop whose influence was more beneficial to the Church.

Alphege assumed the primacy in 1005; and six years later, when Canterbury fell into the hands of the Danes, he was forced to seek sanctuary with his monks within the walls of his Cathedral church. The Danes set fire to the building; and the monks were compelled to emerge. As they did so they were murdered one by one. Alphege was taken prisoner and held to ransom. In the Anglo-Saxon Chronicle the event is described:

then was a captive   where oft before
he who before was   great bliss was seen
of England head   in the fated city
and Christendom –   whence first to us
there might be seen   came Christendom
great wretchedness   and bliss 'fore God. . . .

The good old man refused flatly to appeal for the ransom which would have saved his life. After months of being dragged hither and thither by the Danes, he was set upon in a drunken orgy and pelted with the ox bones left over from a late-night feast. When they saw that he was dead, the Danes seem to have relented a little. They sold his body to the people of London, who gave it honourable burial in St. Paul's Cathedral where it remained until the year 1023. The Chronicle relates:

Siege of Canterbury (*above*) and Abduction of St. Alphege (*below*) by the Danes. Triforium, North Quire aisle, circa 1200.

This year King Canute in London, in St. Paul's minster, gave full leave to Archbishop Ethelnoth, Bishop Britwine, and all God's servants that were with them, that they might take up from the grave the archbishop, St. Alphege. And they did so, on the sixth day before the ides of June; and the illustrious King, and the archbishop, and the diocesan bishops and the earls and very many others, both clergy and laity, carried by ship his holy corpse over the Thames to Southwark. And there they committed the holy martyr to the archbishop and his companions; and they with worthy pomp and sprightly joy carried him to Rochester. There on the third day came the lady Emma with her royal son Hardacanute; and they all with much majesty, and bliss, and songs of praise, carried the holy archbishop into Canterbury, and so brought him gloriously into the Church, on the third day before the ides of June. Afterwards, on the eighth day, the seventeenth before the calends of July, Archbishop Ethelnoth and Bishop Elfsy and Bishop Britwine and all they that were with them, lodged the holy corpse of St. Alphege on the north side of the altar of Christ; to the praise of God, and to the glory of the holy archbishop, and to the everlasting salvation of all those who through his holy body daily seek with earnest heart and all humility. May God Almighty have mercy on all Christian men through the holy intercession of Alphege.

Canute left his crown to be hung from the great rood above the Nave altar, in token of his sorrow for the sin committed by his people: the first but not the last time that a King was to visit the Cathedral as an act of reparation for the murder of an archbishop.

In Eadmer's *Life of St. Anselm*[1] there is a fascinating report of a conversation between Archbishop Lanfranc and the man who was to be his successor in office, on the subject of the canonisation of saints. Lanfranc remarked, not unreasonably, to his old friend: 'These Englishmen among whom we are living have set up for themselves certain saints whom they revere. But sometimes when I turn over in my mind their own accounts of who they were, I cannot help having doubts about their sanctity. Now one of them lies here in the holy church over which by God's will I now preside. He was called Elphege, a good man certainly and in his day archbishop of this place. This man they not only number among the saints, but even among the martyrs, although they do not deny that he was killed, not for professing the name of Christ, but because he refused to buy himself off with money. . . .'

Anselm, who was himself the most convincing in the whole long line of Canterbury's saints, produced some endearingly logical arguments. He pointed out that a martyr is, strictly speaking, one who is killed for his refusal to deny Christ. However: 'It is clear that one who has no hesitation in dying rather than sin against God even in a small matter, would very much rather die than anger God by committing some grave sin. And certainly it appears to be a graver sin to deny Christ than for any lord on earth to injure his men to some extent by taking their money. Much less therefore would he have denied Christ. . . . Moreover, there is the witness of Holy Scripture, as you, Father, very well know, that Christ is both truth and justice; so he who dies for truth and justice dies for Christ. . . . These arguments, Reverend Father, so far as I can see, are what reason itself teaches me to be sound. But it is for your judgement to correct and restrain me if you feel differently. . . .' Lanfranc was convinced. He ordered a history to be written of the life of the Saint, and this was done 'by Osbern, a monk of Canterbury, of happy memory, who wrote it not only in plain prose for reading, but also put it to music for singing; and Lanfranc . . . ordered it to be read and sung in the Church of God. . . .'

[1] *The Life of St. Anselm*. Eadmer. Ed. with introduction, notes and translated by R. W. Southern. Clarendon Press. Oxford 1962.

Lanfranc was the man responsible for the building of the norman Cathedral from which the present one is directly descended, in the sense that there has never been a complete pulling down and rebuilding of it since. The great Archbishop, friend and counsellor of William the Conqueror, was called to England by that monarch. An Italian by birth, he had previously been Abbot of Caen; and he was already seventy years old when he took up his new life. Arriving in Canterbury, he found his Cathedral a charred ruin; the ceremony of his consecration took place in a makeshift hut. Nothing daunted, he set about the task of rebuilding the entire establishment from its foundations, not only literally, but spiritually — for by this time its monks (in so far as they could be described as such at all) had fallen into a lazy, casual way of life. Lanfranc produced his own Constitutions for his new Priory, an amplification of the original Rule of St. Benedict, notable for its combination of mercy with firmness. At the same time he was engaged upon the task of establishing, with some difficulty, the primacy of the see of Canterbury, in the interests of bringing order and discipline and a sense of unity to the English Church. In the archives of the Cathedral is still to be seen the document which sets seal to this achievement. Known as the Accord of Winchester, it is signed with a cross by the Conqueror himself, and by the Papal Legate and six bishops, including Lanfranc. The Archbishop of York admitted defeat: *concedo*, he writes; in contrast to all the others, who write above their signatures, *subscripsi*. So Canterbury Cathedral became, as it remains today, England's premier Cathedral and mother church.

Lanfranc's Cathedral had a Nave of eight bays. This was coterminous with the one we see at present: however, in the sense of its being the 'people's church' (as distinct from the Quire, or domain of the monks), it may be said to have been only half this length: since the 'Quire' occupied the other half. At the west end there was an entrance, then as now, between the twin towers. Presumably, then as now, the most commonly used entrance was the south-west porch. The matutinal altar, as it was called, stood beneath the central tower, which was flanked by two apsidal transepts. Beyond this tower, the church extended for two bays eastwards, ending in three apsidal chapels above the Crypt, the central and largest of which contained the high altar and, behind it, the patriarchal seat. Above the 'Quire' screen (separating the 'people's church' from that of the monks) extended the beam which carried the great rood. This was a Crucifix flanked by the mourning figures of Our Lady and St. John.

Nowadays there is not a great deal left for us to see of Lanfranc's church. That far more of it is still here than meets the eye was proved when, early in this century, holes were drilled in the ashlar casing of the western piers of the central tower, for the purpose of reinforcing them with liquid cement. An original norman shaft with its cushion capital, was then revealed. This may still be seen, high up on the western face of one of the piers, from the landing above the Martyrdom transept. Also from this landing, one can recognise the smaller, more roughly laid, stonework of Lanfranc on the west wall of the transept, to the north. In fact there are bits of this walling in a number of places, if one knows where to look. In the Crypt, the apsidal foundations of one of Lanfranc's three chapels were discovered when the floor was taken up. A curved line inserted into the new flooring in the north aisle indicates the eastern extension of his church.

It was barely twenty years before the east end of Lanfranc's Cathedral was pulled down and rebuilt. Probably it was found to be too small. The rebuilding, which provided the Cathedral with a spacious Quire, leaving the eight bays of the Nave for the use of the laity, so that both they and the monastic community were greatly

The Western Crypt, built in the early part of the twelfth century under the auspices of Prior Ernulf.

benefited as a result, was chiefly the responsibility of one man, who may even have drawn up the plans for it himself. That man was Prior Ernulf. Ernulf was made Abbot of Peterborough in 1114, after which it was left to his successor, Prior Conrad, to supervise the painting and adornment of his work. 'Conrad's glorious Quire' it was eventually called by the monks. But it was Ernulf who built it; and nowadays we speak of what remains of that building as 'Ernulf's chapels' and 'Ernulf's Crypt'.

THOSE WHO enter the Cathedral by the south-west porch, will find themselves looking eastwards up the Nave. This, which will soon be six hundred years old, is the newest part of the Cathedral; and it occupies the site of Lanfranc's Nave, which itself survived three hundred years from the time it was built.

Lanfranc's Nave stood firm through two rebuildings of the eastern end of the church. What we see now is the result of the pulling down of that Nave and its rebuilding in what is known as the Perpendicular style, on the turn of the century, round about the year 1400, under the auspices of Prior Thomas Chillenden, described by a contemporary chronicler as 'the greatest builder of a Prior that ever was in Christes Church'. The architect was Henry Yevele, who was assisted by his partner Stephen Lote. Yevele was employed at Westminster by the Crown: Westminster Hall and part of the Nave of the Abbey are his work. The south-west tower, designed by Thomas Mapilton, was begun in 1424 and took ten years to complete. A few years before this operation was launched, the south-west transept was finished; but its twin to the north, the place of Becket's murder, commonly known as the Martyrdom, remained intact until 1448. Even then it was left with its hallowed floor unraised, and some of the walling which must have looked down upon that dreadful scene deliberately left in place, as if nothing short of necessity could justify its being touched.

Standing at the extreme west end of the Nave, one becomes aware of the extent to which even this part of the building, raised at the close of the middle ages, when religious fervour was beginning to wane and the forces of secularisation to influence the Church (an example of this is the proliferation of secular heraldry which is characteristic of this period) – is an outward expression of the most inward and esoteric aspects of the Christian faith. Because of this,

Opposite
View looking across to the Royal Window from the SW transept. The doorway on the right leads beneath the steps to the Martyrdom, and was the way normally used by the pilgrims, who would enter the Cathedral by the SW porch and proceed up the south aisle to this point. Spanning the two columns is one of the great strainer arches erected by Prior Goldston II to support the weight of the central tower.

it is linked with all the great religious traditions of the world: it is a universal metaphysical statement.

The courtyards of Solomon's temple, leading one, as into the depths of a maze, inwards towards the Holy of Holies which might be entered only by the High Priest — and this because it was his divinely appointed function to enter it, not on account of any moral worthiness inherent in himself — remind us of the ancient and universal idea that *Blessed are the pure in heart for they shall see God.* According to the teachings not only of Christianity but of all the great traditional religions, no human being is so pure as to be worthy of that blinding experience. The corollary of the saying about the pure in heart is Isaiah's cry when he finds himself in the presence of the Lord: *Woe is me, for I am undone, because I am a man of unclean lips.* The approach to the altar of sacrifice on the part of the priest has a complex and profound symbolism attached to it, the essential meaning of which is that man, who is unworthy in himself, is 'made worthy' by the infinite mercy and condescension of God. The symbol of this mystical transaction is the officiating priest. In the Orthodox Church the priests are divided from the laity by the sacred screen called the ikonostasis. In the Catholic Church, there was the sanctuary; but, over and above this division, there existed in every monastic establishment a screen which divided the laity from the monks. A monastic Community was itself regarded as being a symbol of the catching up of the world into God; therefore, symbolically, it was set apart. It is exceedingly difficult for us nowadays to understand the distinction between this ritual 'set-apartness' and the totally unchristian élitism which would have us believe that human beings can be graded according to their worthiness or otherwise to enter the divine presence. That human beings, as such, should be graded in this manner has never been the teaching of the Church; but still the ikonostasis and the screen exist to remind us, symbolically, of our unworthiness 'made worthy' in Christ.

In Canterbury, the view along the central aisle of the Nave,[1] through the small doorway which pierces the screen and directs us to the sensibly darker and spiritually more mysterious regions beyond, recalls to us the ancient idea of the Cave in the Rock. Ceremonies of initiation were frequently enacted in natural caves. Christ was born in a cave, according to one tradition; and according to them all he was buried in one. The cave is a symbol of the womb and, deeper still, of the female principle of receptivity, the human soul opened up to receive the influx from above. This sexual symbolism

Opposite
View looking SE through one of the smaller strainer arches to the altar of the Nave.

Overleaf, left
The Nave looking West. In the great West Window, the central panel at the bottom is the Adam.

Overleaf, right
Nave looking East. The great strainer arch was erected by Prior Goldston II to help bear the weight of the central tower. This picture was taken before Yevele's majestic lines were broken by tilting amplifiers.

[1] The expression 'central aisle' is irresistibly convenient but not strictly correct. Strictly speaking, the 'aisles' are the 'side-walks' only. It is the presence of chairs or pews in churches which has given us the idea of a 'central aisle' or passageway up the centre from west to east.

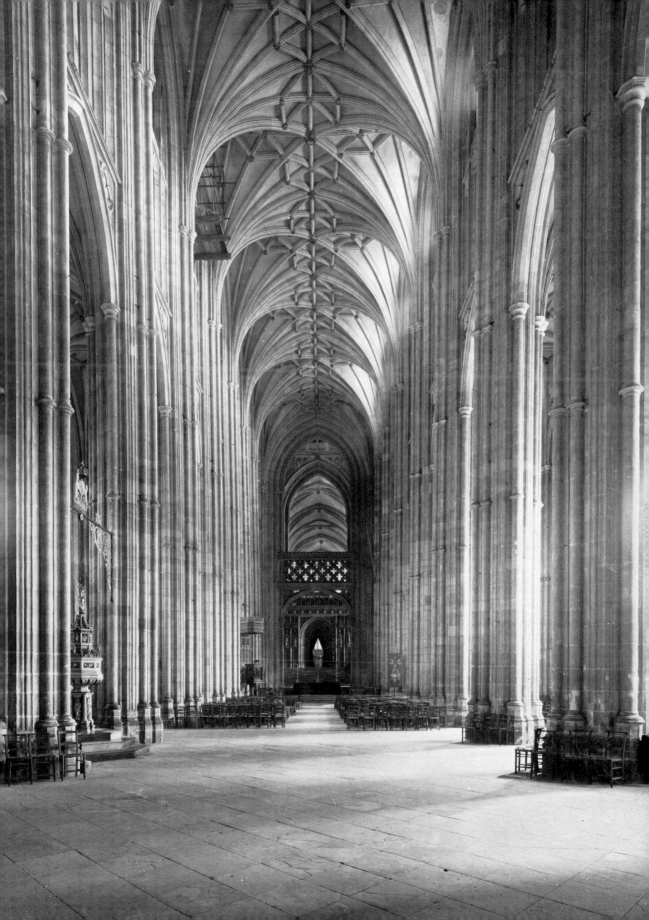

which, if we look for it, is invariably to be found associated with the great centres of religion, is enormously important. It happens to be particularly obvious at Canterbury. And just as the body of a man on a cross or a woman on her bed is unlikely to be absolutely geometrically straight, so the body of the Cathedral is noticeably out of alignment. We can see this as we try to get a fix on the central Cross of the high altar in the Quire, through the opening in the screen. In order to do so, we have to step sideways to the left.

The Nave has what is known as a lierne vault. This style is typical of the perpendicular period, just before the introduction of the fan vaulting which is so much more elaborate. The huge trunk-like columns, with their springing shafts, rise in strong vertical up-thrusts to what seems to be a tremendous height in relation to the breadth of the Nave. John Newman, writing in the *North East and East Kent* volume of *The Buildings of England* makes the following unintentionally ironical observation and comment:

Nothing here to counterbalance the dominant verticals of the piers, for the double-wave is carried up from the ground to vault up and over the clerestory windows. The pier shafts are interrupted by two sets of shaft-rings, but it is a mere whispered interruption.

Yevele's shaft-rings are indeed unobtrusive; even one might argue, aesthetically pleasant. One cannot say the same of the slant-ing amplifiers which nowadays disfigure his Nave, breaking up its perpendiculars again and again in a series of shocks. Our present-day obsession with the amplification of sound is all of a-piece with a corresponding determination to blind ourselves with light. The noise which crackles through these amplifiers and the aesthetic havoc they create all over the Cathedral, combine with the recently installed lighting system to exemplify a general tendency towards artificiality and violence. One prays that future custodians of the building will return to a better understanding of what is in keeping with it.

Yevele's Nave was intended, of course, to be seen in the daytime by the soft light that is mediated through stained and coloured glass. The absence of such glass from most of its windows makes it at all times brighter than it was originally intended to be. The glass of Canterbury Cathedral is still one of the great treasures of Europe; but the collection is by no means intact; successive acts of vandal-ism have depleted it. The great West Window of the Nave and the two smaller windows on either side of it are beautiful still; although even these do not present exactly the same appearance as they did once. The West Window is seen best from a position about half way

Opposite
The south aisle of the Nave as seen from the South Quire aisle.

The bud falls from its stem: plaque in the South Quire aisle. Susanna is buried, with other members of her family, in the Cloisters.

down the Nave; it may also be contemplated at a rather too great distance but without the disadvantage of a crick in the neck, from the steps leading up to the screen.

The Nave itself, once it has been looked at as a whole, tends to be passed over hurriedly, with a glance here and there. This is inevitable on a first visit. Later on, however, it is worthwhile to spend some time exploring it in detail and reading the inscriptions on its monuments. Appropriately, since it was built for the laity, it contains the font. This is an elaborate seventeenth century affair, broken in pieces by the Puritans in 1662, and surprisingly saved by the loving care of William Somner, the Cathedral archivist, who picked up the pieces and preserved them until they could be reassembled when the danger was past. The walls of the Nave are lined with monuments. These are, for the most part, aesthetically uninteresting; but taken as a whole they are full of historical interest and entertainment. Pausing beneath the bust of Orlando Gibbons, who died of a fit of apoplexy while accompanying King Charles the First to Canterbury, to await the arrival of Queen Henrietta Maria from France, we are conscious of a number of worthy citizens of the seventeenth and eighteenth centuries who probably contributed generously to the Cathedral; but then, as we look round, we begin to be aware that the greater part of these monuments are reminders of a phase in our history which nowadays we prefer to forget. Most of them are Victorian, Edwardian, even Georgian, memorials to the Empire-building dead. It is nothing if not strange and pathetic to read these inscriptions to innumerable young men who laid down their lives in places of which we have never heard, not in wars that we know anything about but in creating, establishing and defending that Empire on which 'the sun never set'. We realise as we do so that here is a mentality and a point of view which is further removed from us by far than that of the medieval monks. The experience can be salutary if it forces us to understand that, behind these effusive epitaphs and tasteless marble monuments ('Minerva attending to a soldier with a headache' is Newman's description of one of them) lie stories of sincerity and sacrifice. We are left feeling infinitely sad. Turning for light relief to the recumbent figure of Bishop Broughton near the south-west porch, we may recall that this worthy ecclesiastic provided one of the very few instances of damage inside the Cathedral during the Second World War — when his nose was knocked off. Examining that nose today one can trace only the barest hairline to indicate its replacement.

The Nave did not always present so bare an appearance as it

does today. (Not that one objects to its bareness: one wishes all the chairs could be at least occasionally moved out to throw open Yevele's original concept in all its magnificence.) In the eighteenth century there was a grand clearance of brasses and tombstones when the pavement was taken up and replaced. A number of chantry chapels, which at various times had been situated between the piers, had already been removed. (The object of such chapels was the saying of Masses for the repose of the souls of the dead. Some well-to-do and spiritually provident individual would endow a 'chantry', usually consisting of a chapel with two priests to serve it, for the constant helping along of his soul in its passage through purgatory towards everlasting life. This was a notion unlikely to appeal to any self-respecting protestant.) The bodies of at least four Priors and three Archbishops lie here, beneath our feet. Probably there are many more. In the year 1787, workmen taking up the pavement at the end of the north aisle came upon a leaden coffin containing 'the remains of a body wrapped in a robe of velvet or rich silk fringed with gold'. The inscription ran *Hic requiescit venerabilis memorie Theobaldus Cantuarie archiepiscopus Britanie*. This was the site of the Lady Chapel in Lanfranc's Cathedral. The monk Gervase, who left us an eye-witness account of the burning and rebuilding of the Quire in the seventies of the twelfth century, describes how it was found necessary at that time to interfere with

Major General Charles Norman leads a wreath-laying delegation (in the background, Mr. Gill, Keeper of the Gate): a post-war glimpse of a world on the verge of extinction, a world which in its day was an integral part of the life of the Cathedral and its Precincts.

In 1908 Eric Gill was asked to design a plaque in the Nave commemorating one Colonel Ravenhill who died at Wynberg. The work was evidently meant to be anonymous, but Gill found his own way of signing it. Not shown in this photograph, a tiny 'A' in front of the 'E' makes the initials: A.E.R.Gill. (For observation of the 'A' I am indebted to the sharp eyes of Edmund de Waal.)

certain tombs, including that of this great Archbishop.

When they opened the tomb of Archbishop Theobald, which was built of marble slabs, and came to his sarcophagus, the monks who were present expecting to find his body reduced to dust, brought wine and water to wash his bones. But when the lid of the sarcophagus was raised, he was found entire and rigid, and still subsisting in bones and nerves, skin and flesh, but somewhat attenuated. The bystanders marvelled at this sight, and placing him upon a bier, they carried him as they had done Lanfranc, to the vestiarium, to await the decision of the convent. But the rumour began to spread among the people, and already, for this unwarranted incorruption, many called him St. Theobald. He was exhibited to some who desired to see him, and they helped to spread the tale among the rest.

He was thus raised from his sepulchre in the nineteenth year from his death, his body being incorrupted, and his silk vestments entire. And by the decision of the convent was buried in a leaden coffin before the altar of St. Mary, in the nave of the church. . . .[1]

The dust and a few bones belonging to Archbishop Lanfranc were re-interred at the same time in the chapel of St. Martin in the north quire aisle. The Community had consulted together, wondering 'what should be done with so great a Father'. But when they came to examine him 'his very bones were consumed with rottenness'. Thus poor Lanfranc was not credited with being a saint. In the end, however, it would seem that we are all of us dust: 'these remains', according to the contemporary account of Archbishop Theobald's eventual reappearance, 'were much decayed'.

MOST PEOPLE, on leaving the Nave mount the steps behind the altar and look back at the West Window, with its Kings and prophets, patriarchs and saints. The lower half of the window contains thirteen figures from what is known as the Genealogical series, depicting those patriarchs of the Old Testament who were said to have been the ancestors of Christ. Originally this series was in the clerestory of the Quire; now what remains of it has been collected in this window, and in the great window of the south transept which can also be seen from the steps. The oldest glass in the Cathedral, it is late twelfth century in date. The remaining panels in the West Window date from the fourteenth and fifteenth centuries, the row of Kings in particular being of considerable beauty and interest; but the Patriarchs stand out above all in unrivalled magnifi-

[1] Quoted from *Architectural History of Some English Cathedrals. Part 1.* Rev. Robert Willis M.A., F.R.S. Paul P. B. Minet. Chicheley. 1972.

cence. In the centre is Adam delving, a reference to the expulsion from paradise, when the Lord condemned him to eat bread 'in the sweat of thy face'. This is understandably the most famous panel of glass in the Cathedral. Where the other figures are static, this is an action picture, a startling combination of realism with myth. Here is the archetypal Adam; and here is a man digging in a field, stripped to the waist, a second implement hanging beside him on the branch of a tree. The colours are blue, green, yellow and ruby red. Beside it, and in the transept window, the sons of Adam in the direct line are seated squarely on their patriarchal thrones, their names inscribed behind their heads: Sem, Aram, Jeconias, Rhesa, Ozias, Enoch, Abia, Abraham — and the rest. The figures seem to quiver and vibrate. They possess the statuesque dignity of a Henry

Left
In the sweat of thy brow
shalt thou eat bread . . .
Adam in exile from Eden.
Twelfth century panel from
the great West Window.

Right
The 'Adam' seen from the
back, showing the corrosion
which has necessitated the
work of restoration.

Moore, combined with a living intensity which cannot easily be found elsewhere in the field of art. (Thinking of Chartres, one realises that, strangely enough, it is in the art of the twelfth and thirteenth century glaziers that one finds this quality of burning livingness as nowhere else.)

In the Second World War the Cathedral might well have lost its entire treasure of medieval glass. That it did not do so, was due to a great extent to the foresight of Dean Hewlett Johnson, who insisted upon its removal at an early stage. After the war it took six years to put it back. In 1973 Mr. Frederick Cole, an eminent artist in stained glass, was put in charge of a new and greatly improved Cathedral workshop. To him has fallen the task of being responsible for the cleaning and restoration of glass which has recently been discovered to be rapidly disintegrating as a result of atmospheric pollution and damp. This is a problem which requires for its solution a fund of scientific and technical knowledge which has only lately become available: knowledge, moreover, which is being daily augmented at the present time by concentrated research. Mr. Cole, when he is good enough to spare the time – from his own leisure, never from his work – explains to the visitor one infinitesimal part of that work and sends him away feeling humbled in his ignorance. Tentatively, in the doorway, the visitor pauses and asks: 'Mr. Cole – this idea that people have about the medieval glass – that *blue* for instance – did they really have a secret method of producing it which we shall never be able to repeat?' The Master glazier smiles gently at this old wives' tale and promptly disposes of it. On the contrary, he says, we can produce all the colours they used and many more of which they never dreamed. Not, of course, that he does not profoundly respect their work: his life is dedicated to the preservation of it. He is merely being a realist. Who is the uninitiated ignoramus to go on wondering if – perhaps – after all he is mistaken in this one respect? And yet. . . .

AIR RAIDS and atmospheric pollution may have threatened Canterbury's glass; but by far the most effectual of its enemies were the Puritan fanatics. Facing the Window of the Patriarchs, across the width of the Cathedral, is the Royal Window of the north-west transept. Apart from the tracery lights and a band of heraldic angels carrying shields, there is left in this enormous perpendicular window only the middle band, depicting King Edward IV and his family in kneeling attitudes, apparently praying to the Tudor Arms. These royal figures, donors of the window, originally occupied the bottom row but one: their present position, indeed their very existence, being due to the fact that, as mere human beings, they failed to give offence.

It is unfair and inaccurate to blame the Protector himself for the shocking scenes which took place in Canterbury Cathedral as a result of his Ordinance prohibiting 'Idolatrous Monuments'. The trouble was caused, in the main, by drunken soldiery and by gangs of near-psychotic individuals having a roaring good day out. A certain Richard Culmer, known in the city as Blue Dick, who was actually a minister of religion (and was later installed as a 'six preacher' at the Cathedral, being described as 'a godly and orthodox divine') made himself personally responsible for the destruction of the Royal Window. Availing himself of the city ladder, he climbed up behind it with a pike. It is to Blue Dick himself that we owe a detailed description of the beauties he sent crashing to the pavement:

In that window was now a picture of God the Father and of Christ, besides a large Crucifix and the picture of the Holy Ghost, in the form of a Dove, and of the twelve Apostles; and in that window were seven large pictures of the Virgin Marie, in seven several glorious appearances, as of the Angells lifting her into heaven, and the Sun, Moon and stars under her feet. . . .

Culmer seems to have taken particular exception to a representation of Becket: 'most rarely pictured . . . with Cope, Rochet, Mitre, Crosier and all his Pontificalibus'. With glee he informs us that, while 'the Cathedrallists cryed out again for their great Diana, hold your hands, holt, holt', he himself was 'ratling down proud Becket's glassy bones' — at which point some right-minded citizen came up behind him and expressed the understandable hope that he might break his neck.

Blue Dick, however, was not acting alone on this occasion. He tells us:

Many window-images or pictures in glass were destroyed that day and many idolls of stone, thirteen representing Christ and the twelve Apostles standing over the West door of the Quire were all hewed down and twelve more at the North Door of the Quire and twelve Mytred Saints sate aloft over the West door of the Quire, which were all cast down headlong, and some fell on their heads and their myters brake their necks. . . . Many other images were defaced . . . several pictures of God the Father, of Crucifixes and men praying to Crucifixes and to the Virgin Mary; and images lay on the tombs with eyes and hands lifted up, and right over them was pictured God the Father, embracing a Crucifix to which the

Image seemed to pray.[1] There was a Cardinall's hat as red as blood, painted in the highest window in that Cathedral within Bell Harry steeple over the quire door . . . which hat had not so much respect showed it as Cardinall Wolsey's hat had at Court, it was not bowed down to but rattled down . . . the last execution against the Idols in that Cathedral was done in the Cloysters, divers crucifixes and mitred saints were battered in pieces there: St. Dunstan's image pulling the Devil by the nose with a pair of tongs was pulled down Devil and all. When the Cathedral men heard that Ordinance of Parliament against Idolotrous Monuments was to be put into execution, they covered a complete Crucifix in the Sermon House with thin boards and painted them to preserve their Crucifix, but their jugling was found out and the Crucifix demolisht.

Only a year before these scenes took place, the Cathedral had been violently assaulted by troops. The vice-Dean described this event in a letter, as follows:

When the soldiers, entering the church and quire, giant-like began to fight against God Himself, overthrew the Communion table, tore the velvet cloth from before it, defaced the goodly screen of tabernacle work, violated the monuments of the dead, spoiled the organs, broke down the ancient rails and seats with the brazen eagle that did support the Bible, forced open the cupboards of the singing-men, rent some of their surplices, gowns and Bibles and carried away others, mangled all our service books and books of Common Prayer, bestrewing the whole pavement with leaves thereof – a miserable spectacle to all good eyes. But as if all this had been too little to satisfy the fury of some indiscreet zealots among them (for many did abhor what was done already) they further expressed their malice upon the arras hangings of the quire, wherein observing the figures of Christ (I tremble to express their blasphemies), one said 'Here is Christ', and swore that he would stab Him, which they did accordingly so far as the figures were capable thereof . . . and . . . finding another statue of Christ in the Frontispiece of the south-gate they discharged against it forty shot at the least. . . .

It is clear from the context that the figure referred to was the one which occupied the central niche in the facade of Christ Church Gate; further shots, meanwhile, were expended upon the little crucifix, part of the representation of what was known as the Altar of the Swords Point, still to be seen in its battered state above the south-west porch. Less easy game for these madmen was the tremendous Angel on the gable of the south transept, which was pulled to the ground by the exertions of a hundred men, after having been somehow lassooed with a rope.

One marvels that anything was left.

T HE 'WEST door of the Quire' in Culmer's account refers to the

Above
Sadly mutilated by the Puritans, this little representation of the altar *ad punctum ensis* (of the Sword's Point) is still to be seen above the SW porch. At the foot of the altar are the two pieces of Le Breton's shattered sword which were preserved as relics.

Opposite
The Screen of the Six Kings divides the Quire from the Nave.

[1] This may refer to the now defaced painting on the tester above the tomb of the Black Prince.

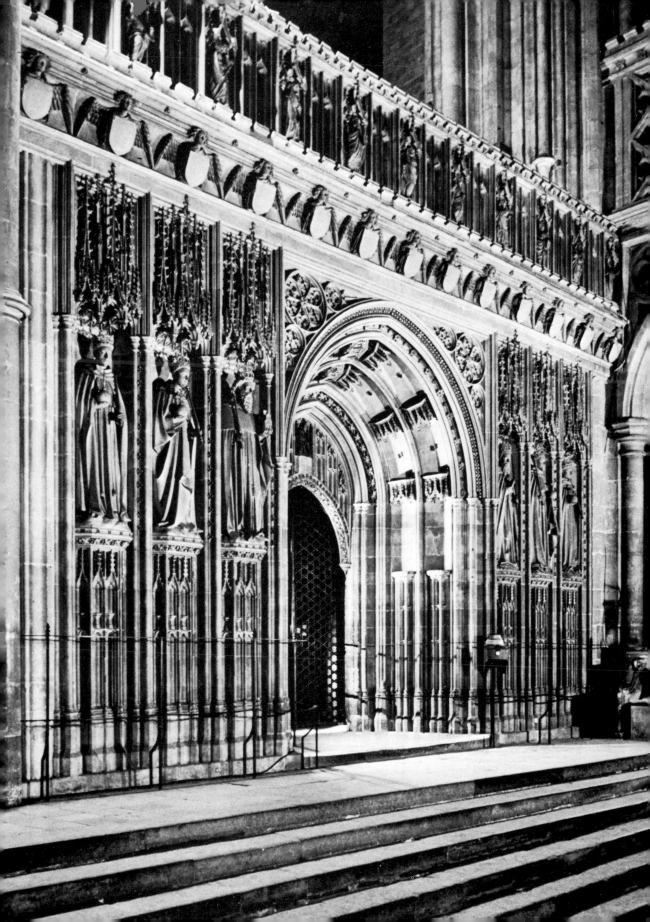

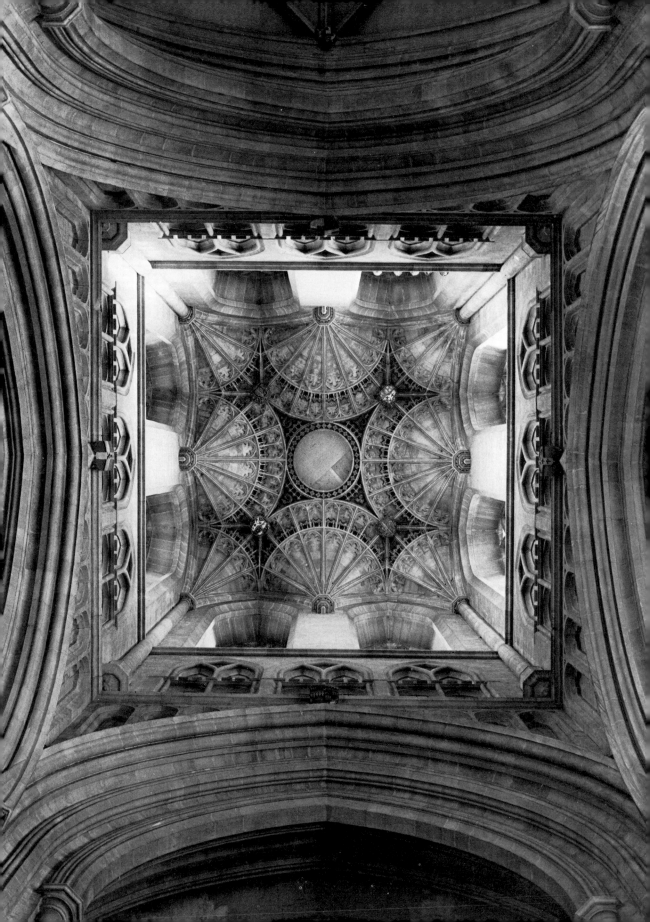

pulpitum or Quire screen. When the 'twelve mitred saints' were 'cast down headlong' from this screen, there were left in its principal niches the figures of Six Kings. Their identity is uncertain; but they are generally designated as Henry V, Richard II, Ethelbert, Edward the Confessor, Henry IV and Henry VI. Above them is a band of Angels carrying shields. Dr. William Urry (who probably has a more extensive knowledge of Canterbury Cathedral than any other living person at the present time) writes [1] fondly of 'the thirteen superb angels' heads along the top of the choir screen. They are obviously portraits of beautiful young girls around the Court. My favourite is the fourth from the right. The whole screen needs detailed treatment. [2] There are masses of human heads on it and what must be the most delicate Gothic tracery anywhere in stone.'

Standing before the archway which pierces the screen, on the top of the steps, the visitor would be well advised to look straight up above his head. One hundred and twenty-six feet up, the restored and re-painted fan vaulting of the lantern of the central tower, creates a pattern of flowerlike delicacy, enclosing a kind of mandala on a blue ground. This ground is four-pointed like a star: on its four points, gold against blue, are the letters TGP (Thomas Goldston, Prior) and three gold stones arranged like a clover leaf, the second Prior Goldston's punning rebus. In alignment with the central tower, on either side, are the two western transepts. The one to the south

Tiny faces carved on the canopies of the Six Kings.

Opposite
The lantern of Bell Harry as seen from the steps above the Nave altar. In the four corners are the letters TGP (Thomas Goldston Prior) and the three gold stones which are the second Prior Goldston's punning rebus.

Bell Harry is tolled by a verger for the death of King George V in January 1936.

[1] In a letter to the author.
[2] i.e. in print, *not* from cleaners and restorers!

has, in addition to the Window of the Patriarchs, an equally imposing (as regards its size and traceries, not its glass) Perpendicular
West Window, with an overall scheme of glass by the nineteenth
century artist Christopher Whall, who was strongly influenced by
Rossetti and Burne-Jones. It is a sad comment on the modern glass
which has been introduced into the Cathedral since the Second
World War, that this pale reflection of the Pre-Raphaelites should
seem positively beautiful and meaningful in comparison with it.
(One can only hope that a new generation of glaziers will redress the
balance: a window in the south quire aisle is about to be thrown open
to competition, and one holds one's breath.) Facing the Whall

The fourth angel from the
right on the screen of the
Six Kings.

window is St. Michael's Chapel, dominated by the tomb of Margaret
Holland and her two husbands. Detailed consideration of this chapel,
or rather of this tomb, must be postponed: it belongs to the story
of the remarkable family party which was held in the Cathedral by
the deceased members of the family of King Edward III.

'Excuse me', comes the familiar question, as one makes one's way
through the crowds of visitors, wearing one's badge as a Cathedral
guide perhaps, or contriving in some indefinable manner to look as if
one owned the place (everyone who has anything to do with the
Cathedral succumbs to this temptation, more or less; it is part of a
defence mechanism against the vergers — who really almost do) —

Norman doorway leading
from the Martyrdom
transept to Ernulf's Crypt.
The diamond pattern on the
wall is typically roman-
esque.

'excuse me, but could you tell me where Becket was murdered?' One points the way, a little reluctantly because there are better things to see; and, no, there is no blood, you must understand that it all looks quite different now, the norman transept was pulled down in the fifteenth century and rebuilt. (Not to mention the activities of one Benedict, who carried off a sizeable portion of the flooring to the monastery of Peterborough, of which he had just been made Abbot — in return for his services as likely as not: he would not have been the first to qualify for ecclesiastical preferment by carrying out a commission of this sort.)

The 'place of the murder', commonly known as the Martyrdom, is the north-west transept. In Becket's time this was divided into two storeys. On each floor there was a central pillar and an apsidal chapel at the eastern end, the chapel on the ground floor being dedicated to St. Benedict. A flight of steps led up into the north quire aisle. Of all this there is virtually nothing left to be seen, apart from the staircase turret and the lower part of the wall on the corner by the entrance to the Crypt. The chapel leading out of the transept is fan vaulted, with an entrance screen of the same period in elaborate stonework. This is known as the Deans' Chapel on account of its somewhat overpowering monuments to a succession of seventeenth century Deans. In the transept itself, the prone figures of two Arch-bishops take up the length of the north wall. One of these is carved in bog oak. The wood is dark and hard and smooth. An impulse to slide one's fingers along it leads to thoughts of the man whose body it represents. Archbishop Peckham was a member of the Order of St. Francis. He suffered from melancholy: in a letter, addressed to the Prior of the time, from one of his associates, he is described as having become unapproachable and morose. Perhaps he missed his gentle Brotherhood, not far away in their Friary above the stream. Well he might have done. The archiepiscopal palace of Canterbury was seldom a haven of relaxation for its occupants.

The monument to the east of Peckham is that of Archbishop Warham, whose chantry chapel used to lead out of this transept into the slype which divides it from the Chapter House. The site of the altar of this chapel is at present occupied by a kitchen sink. A faintly surrealist quality is added to the breath-taking sacrilege of such an arrangement when we learn that the Archbishop's body was probably interred beneath the altar rather than beneath the monument.

So we come to St. Thomas. A great deal has yet to be explained about St. Thomas. Scholarly books have been written attempting to

The Bog Oak Archbishop:
a mutilated figure in smooth
stone-hard bog oak
represents Archbishop John
Peckham in the Martyrdom
transept. The stonework
above the arcading is
Lanfranc's.

prove that both he and the King were secret adherents of the 'old
religion' of magic and witchcraft and ritual sacrifice, which demanded at regular intervals the death of the King or his substitute.
These theories are unproven; and nowadays they seem to go un-
noticed. However, they serve to indicate a certain atmosphere surrounding both the murder and the subsequent cult. How could the
man have been so sure that he was going to be murdered, precisely
then, at the winter solstice — so sure that he warned the people of
Canterbury, in a sermon preached at the Cathedral on Christmas
Eve, of his approaching death? Why did they murder him in so

peculiar and horrible a manner, by slicing off the crown of his head? And so on. It is not our business here to rummage about in the depths of esoteric lore for the purpose of producing an argument. For those who are at all familiar with such lore its connections with the story are sufficiently obvious. They may or may not be entirely fortuitous.

Thomas Becket was born at a house in Cheapside in the year 1118. His father was a city merchant of norman descent. A turn in the fortunes of the young Thomas came in his middle twenties when he was introduced into the household of Theobald, Archbishop of Canterbury, in the capacity of a clerk. He seems to have become a priest by stages which proceeded in accordance with the demands of his worldly career. In Theobald's service he was ordained as a deacon. When, as a result of the Archbishop's influence with the King, he was appointed Chancellor of England, leaping into high office almost (as it seems to us) overnight, he made no further move to become a fully fledged priest: on the contrary, he became a great deal more worldly than Theobald had been led to anticipate. King Henry II and his Chancellor enjoyed one another's company to the utmost. Henry was a complex character, but his contemporaries are united in describing him as charming, outgoing and of a generous disposition. He delighted in magnificent display and lavish entertainments. He and Thomas rode and hunted and feasted together. Thomas enjoyed enormous power; and showed no inclination to restrain his royal master in his frequent clashes with the Church. The story is infinitely fascinating: we shall never know what complexities of the human psyche lie behind it. One is inclined to feel that the very intensity of the King's affection for his friend was a factor in their subsequent violent quarrels and estrangements. It was said of King Henry that his feelings never changed towards anyone whom he had either hated or loved. As for Thomas, when he found that he was to be appointed to fill the exalted position which the death of his old master Theobald had left vacant, it is said that he remonstrated with the King. One wonders exactly why. It is as if he were trying to say to his friend: 'You do not know me. There is more than one Thomas. Stick to the one you have; and do not deliberately bring into being his opposite. Thomas the Chancellor is not the same person as Thomas the Archbishop.'

Henry, however, not unnaturally supposed that, with Thomas at Canterbury, he could do as he liked with the Church. We do not know whether Thomas, when he found himself ordained priest and immediately afterwards made Archbishop, underwent some overwhelming spiritual experience; or whether he was simply one of those complicated characters who can switch from one personality to another as circumstances dictate. In any case he seems to have decided immediately that his first loyalty was no longer to the King but to the Pope. One feels, too, that for the first time in his life, he acknowledged unreservedly his fealty to God. Perhaps, after all, he was conscious of the removal of an underlying conflict. Perhaps, as T. S. Eliot has suggested, he set out to be a saint.

The character and motivations of the Archbishop have more to do with the Cathedral, having entered into its very stones as have the passions and prayers of all those who have lived in intimate association with it, than the ramifications of the fearful battle between Church and State which was fought out during his period of office and resulted in his death. Therefore we shall dispense with a discussion of the Constitutions of Clarendon and the rights and wrongs of hauling up an offending cleric before a secular court. Our business is with Thomas on his return to Canterbury after six years of exile in France. He arrived at the port of Sandwich and was greeted by a crowd of fisherfolk, who rushed into the fringes of the sea to drag in his boat, calling for his blessing as they did so. Thomas was in a cold fury that day; but he blessed these poor people with fatherly love. He was a priest before anything else.

T. S. Eliot has the people cry out:

Evil the wind, and bitter the sea, and grey the sky, grey
grey grey.
O Thomas, return, Archbishop; return, return to France.
Return. Quickly. Quickly. Leave us to perish in quiet.
You come with applause, you come with rejoicing, but you come
bringing death into Canterbury:
A doom on the house, a doom on yourself, a doom on the world.
We do not wish anything to happen.

Obviously they said nothing of the kind; but this passage, as indeed the whole play from which it is taken, brings out the sinister and inevitable aspect of the sequence of events. Despite his recent (and not over-enthusiastic) 'reconciliation' with the King, Thomas had sent messengers ahead of him bearing excommunications to be distributed right and left. The principal cause of his indignation was the usurpation of his functions in his absence by the Archbishop of York. The King's eldest son had been crowned by this prelate as a kind of understudy to the King. The fact that Thomas would have had to practise bi-location in order to perform the ceremony himself seems not to have weighed with him at all. He returned to his city and his Cathedral, seemingly intoxicated with the prospect of martyrdom in the cause of the primacy of Canterbury over York. His triumphal progress was later to be likened inevitably to the entry of Christ into Jerusalem on the eve of His death. Like his Master, Thomas was openly foretelling his own death, speaking of it as if it were something pre-ordained from which there could be no question of trying to escape. And yet we are asked to believe that what actually happened was the result of a very tiny incident.

King Henry was in France with his Court. When he heard of the excommunications which had been handed out to every one of the bishops who had been present at his son's coronation, he was not unnaturally indignant. Plans were made in haste. The King was determined to discipline his unruly Archbishop, if necessary by imprisonment. One can hardly imagine that murder was seriously in his thoughts. Amid all the crudity and violence of the times, there was no one from the King downwards who did not stand in some awe of the power of the Church (had this not been so, the distribution of excommunications would not have seemed so enormously important). One did not simply murder the Archbishop of Canterbury as if he were some mere baron or knight who was making himself a nuisance.

We are asked to believe that four knights of the King's Court, after consulting together hastily in secret, returned to England and forthwith murdered the Archbishop, in his own Cathedral and in the bloodiest, most revolting manner imaginable, committing the most appalling sacrilege in an age when sacrilege was the most appalling of all crimes, for no better reason than that one day the King lost his temper and shouted at the top of his voice: 'Is there no one who will rid me of this low-born clerk?' A more unlikely tale has seldom found its way into a history book. But there it is; and since it is all that we have got, we had better make the best of it.

The very names of the four knights seem as if they belong to the world of myth. Reginald Fitzurse, Hugh de Moreville, William de Tracy, Richard le Breton, they roll off the tongue as if they had been invented by some bard, rather than being the names of actual individuals who took part in an historical event. There are moments when one almost wonders whether the whole business ever happened in the world we inhabit. But it did happen. It happened in the north-west transept of Canterbury Cathedral at sundown on December 29th in the year 1170. Thomas, the Archbishop, Primate of England, was murdered as he stood, face to face, in his own church, by four armed men who sliced off the top of his head and

Opposite
The patriarch Enoch, from the twelfth century series of 'Geneological Windows' depicting the ancestors of Christ. The hand of the Lord prepares to grasp His servant, illustrating the story that Enoch was translated bodily into Heaven.

scooped out his brains and spread them on the pavement, leaving him lying there in the dark, deserted for a time by monks and citizens alike.

He had been as brave as any human being could be. The knights had challenged him first in his palace; then, when they departed temporarily, he had vested himself for the Evening Office and proceeded, with a few attendants, through the Cloisters, to join the Community already in the church. It was as he was ascending the steps into the Quire, that a violent commotion was heard outside, caused by the approach of the four knights with their gang of mercenaries and thugs, the riff-raff of the countryside which by this time was clattering in their wake.

The story of what followed is familiar to us all from innumerable factual accounts. We shall be no further from the truth of that story if we read it in the version of a great poet, another Thomas, who took the actual words of the Archbishop (as those words have come down to us, reported by eye-witnesses) and transposed them faithfully into verse:

PRIESTS
Bar the door. Bar the door.
The door is barred.
We are safe. We are safe.
They dare not break in.
They cannot break in. They have not the force.
We are safe. We are safe.

THOMAS
Unbar the doors! throw open the doors!
I will not have the house of prayer, the church of Christ,
The sanctuary, turned into a fortress.
The Church shall protect her own, in her own way, not
As oak and stone; stone and oak decay,
Give no stay, but the Church shall endure.
The Church shall be open, even to our enemies. Open
     the door!

FIRST PRIEST
My Lord! these are not men, these come not as men come, but
Like maddened beasts. They come not like men, who
Respect the sanctuary, who kneel to the Body of Christ,
But like beasts. You would bar the door
Against the lion, the leopard, the wolf or the boar,
Why not more
Against beasts with the souls of damned men, against men
Who would damn themselves to beasts. My Lord! My Lord!

THOMAS
Unbar the door!
You think me reckless, desperate and mad.
You argue by results, as this world does,
To settle if an act be good or bad.
You defer to the fact. For every life and every act
Consequence of good and evil can be shown.
And as in time results of many deeds are blended
So good and evil in the end become confounded.
It is not in time that my death shall be known;
It is out of time that my decision is taken
If you call that decision
To which my whole being gives entire consent.
I give my life
To the Law of God above the Law of Man.
Unbar the door! Unbar the door!
We are not here to triumph by fighting, by stratagem, or
    by resistance,
Not to fight with beasts as men. We have fought the beast
And have conquered. We have only to conquer
Now, by suffering. This is the easier victory.
Now is the triumph of the Cross, now
Open the door! I command it. OPEN THE DOOR!

(*The door is opened. The* KNIGHTS *enter . . .*)

PRIESTS
This way, my Lord! Quick. Up the Stair. To the roof.
    To the crypt. Quick. Come. Force him.

KNIGHTS
Where is Becket, the traitor to the King?
Where is Becket, the meddling priest?
Come down Daniel to the lions' den,
Come down Daniel for the mark of the beast.

Are you washed in the blood of the Lamb?
Are you marked with the mark of the beast?
Come down Daniel to the lions' den,
Come down Daniel and join in the feast.

Where is Becket the Cheapside brat?
Where is Becket the faithless priest?
Come down Daniel to the lions' den,
Come down Daniel and join in the feast.

THOMAS
It is the just man who
Like a bold lion, should be without fear.
I am here.
No traitor to the King. I am a priest,

Opposite
'Becket's Doorway' leading
from the Cloisters into the
Martyrdom transept.
Thirteenth century arcading
is rudely overlaid by the
spouting shafts of Prior
Chillenden's vault. An early
fifteenth century doorway
completes the general
discomfort. And yet . . .?

A Christian, saved by the blood of Christ,
Ready to suffer with my blood.
This is the sign of the Church always,
The sign of blood. Blood for blood.
His blood given to buy my life,
My blood given to pay for his death,
My death for His death.

FIRST KNIGHT
Absolve all those you have excommunicated.

SECOND KNIGHT
Resign the powers you have arrogated.

THIRD KNIGHT
Restore to the King the money you appropriated.

FIRST KNIGHT
Renew the obedience you have violated.

THOMAS
For my Lord I am now ready to die
That his Church may have peace and liberty.
Do with me as you will, to your hurt and shame;
But none of my people, in God's name,
Whether layman or clerk, shall you touch.
This I forbid.

KNIGHTS
Traitor! traitor! traitor!

THOMAS
You, Reginald, three times traitor you:
Traitor to me as my temporal vassal,
Traitor to me as your spiritual lord,
Traitor to God in desecrating His Church.

FIRST KNIGHT
No faith do I owe to a renegade,
And what I owe shall now be paid.

THOMAS
   Now to Almighty God, to the Blessed Mary ever Virgin, to the blessed John the Baptist, the holy apostles Peter and Paul, to the blessed martyr Denys, and to all the Saints, I commend my cause and that of the Church.

   When the petrified monks at last came creeping down with their candles held aloft they found a bloody mess. It is sometimes forgotten that one of Eliot's greatest lines, best known as he used it for the second time in his *Four Quartets*, belonged originally to his play about the murder of Thomas Becket:

Human kind cannot bear very much reality.

Just occasionally, as one crosses the north-west transept, a flicker of the reality of that evening, eight centuries ago, returns to make one catch one's breath.

T HE QUIRE seems to fly forwards and upwards, its presbytery oddly nipped in and rising steeply to the High Altar, beyond which the Trinity Chapel (the place of the Shrine) expands like a bubble half blown up. Built in the seventies of the twelfth century, in the Early Gothic style of the Ile de France, it reminds those who have been there of the Cathedral at Sens, the native city of its architect. The style is transitional, with semi-pointed arches and a sexpartite vault at a height of sixty-nine feet. The soft grey-brown colour of the stone contrasts with the darker brown of the frequently recurring marble shafts.[1] The total effect is infinitely beautiful, infinitely religious. An old Turkish Sufi, knowing little or nothing of Christianity, recently visited the Cathedral and sat for a long time near the crossing of the Quire, oblivious of the swarming visitors and the echoing talk. Afterwards he said 'The men who built this place were in possession of the ancient gnosis.'

Here in the Quire the Community chanted the Hours which redeem the passing time. Here they celebrated Mass. The Monastic Office divides time octagonally, marking the twenty-four hours eight times by eight liturgical services called Matins, Lauds, Prime, Terce, Sext, Nones, Vespers, Compline: these services consisting of the chanting of psalms and passages from the scriptures, together with certain formal prayers and responses, arranged in accordance with the seasons and feast days of the Church.

The inner meaning of the Religious Life, as this was conceived of in the middle ages, the heyday of its influence, was that of a Community set apart to mirror the Divine Order, in a way that was not practically feasible for the larger community of secular society — although this too was supposed to reflect in a dimmer, more diffused manner the pattern set by the monks. The function of the Religious Orders, bound by the three vows of Poverty, Chastity and Obedience and the daily round of prayer and work, was held to be nothing less than that of participating in the redemption of time, the catching up of the world into the Order of Creation in God. If the actual Religious

[1] The present dark chocolate colour of many of these shafts is due to an overlay of some kind: where this is absent a contrast remains but is less obtrusive and presumably more in accordance with the intention of the architect.

Communities were frequently very far indeed from realising their sublime vocation, this unworthiness tended to be overlooked in a society imbued with the idea that all men are unworthy all the time. An intense preoccupation with 'worthiness' is typically protestant; the tendency to fling their unworthiness in their faces is typical of the present-day humanist attitude to Catholics. In medieval times one accepted one's sinful state, took out certain insurances against Hell, and got along happily enough.

The daily work of such an establishment was considered to be the *Opus Dei*, the praises of God. The medieval idea of the tribute due to the liege lord through all the ranks of an hierarchical society, was carried over into the sphere of religion; indeed it had its origin in that sphere: the structure of society and the structure of Creation were regarded as corresponding the one to the other, as indeed the entire world was built up of correspondences wherever one looked. The Religious Orders had the task of paying the dues that were owed to the Creator, on their own account and on behalf of everyone else. Of course the monks were obliged to work hard in the ordinary sense. A large establishment such as the Priory of Christ Church would have numerous servants; but the tasks of administration were exceedingly onerous, and there were all kinds of other duties to be performed and works to be carried out. All this was a necessary part of preserving oneself and one's brethren in existence – for the sake of the real work which constituted the justification of that existence. This vision of a society united in the offering of prayer, with the monks as it were performing the part of the mouth which must actually utter that prayer, is part of an even greater vision of the inter-relatedness of the living and the dead, the praying community on earth upholding the departed souls by their intercession and by the Sacrifice of the Mass, united with and dependent upon the prayers of the saints. This vision in its wholeness is what the great Anglican theologian Charles Williams (whose name is connected with Canterbury Cathedral through the play which he wrote for performance in the Chapter House) was in the habit of referring to as the Coinherence. Another name for it is simply the Church.

We can picture the monks as they came from their living quarters on the north side of the Cathedral, back and forth, back and forth, by day and by night. Generation would give place to generation, but the work would go on. The daily celebration of the Mass, the daily Office; and behind all this, according as each individual was capable of it, the prayer of the heart. In winter it must have been excruciatingly cold and uncomfortable to have to get up in the middle of the

Opposite
William's Quire looking West in the direction of the Nave.

night and pad across from the Dormitory to the Cathedral in one's sandalled feet. Half way between these two points were the wash-basins, where one was supposed to pause and perform at least a token ablution before proceeding to the church. Besides being cold, the nights would have frequently been pitch dark until one could light up a candle or a torch. We who have forgotten the impact of darkness, have forgotten also the tenderness and comfort of flickering lights. The Quire must have looked strange and almost supernaturally beautiful by candlelight, as the sacred psalmody of the Church was flung from side to side in a rhythm like the waves of the sea.

Opposite
William's Quire looking East in the direction of the Trinity Chapel.

Below
Alfred Deller, greatest of all counter-tenors, whose voice was discovered by Sir Michael Tippett, while he was still an unknown lay-clerk at Canterbury Cathedral towards the end of World War II.

FROM THE musical history of our country emerge two names which are closely associated with Canterbury Cathedral: Alfred Deller and Thomas Tallis. Both men were lay-clerks at Canterbury, the one in the sixteenth century, the other in the twentieth. Alfred Deller, in our own time, has been instrumental in bringing about a great revival of interest in the English composers of the sixteenth and seventeenth centuries: one of whom was Tallis. There is a link, not only between these two, but between both and those medieval brethren who transposed the visual beauty of their Quire into the sacred sound of the Gregorian plainsong chant. The music which Tallis composed for the Church (which continues to be used regularly in Canterbury Cathedral) and that which Deller most cares to sing, are close in spirit to the middle ages in spite of being stylistically different; because both are essentially religious and Christian, in the deepest sense in which those words are capable of being used. Such music is passionless and anonymous; and yet no human passion could be so intense, and no expression of human individuality so tender and intimate. The voice of Alfred Deller, which possesses a quality setting it apart from that of all other contemporary counter-tenors (none of whom would have come into existence as such had he not been responsible single-handed – or single-voiced one should say perhaps – for reviving this voice and teaching the correct method of producing it) – this voice strikes a note in the heart which vibrates on the level not of the emotions but of the spirit.

Sir Michael Tippett, who discovered Alfred Deller when the latter was still an unknown lay-clerk in Canterbury during the Second World War, defines the counter-tenor voice as 'a male alto of what would be regarded now as exceptional range and facility' and says

of it: 'It is like no other sound in music, and few other musical sounds are intrinsically so musical.' One associates it with Purcell and the heyday of English music at the time of the Restoration. 'Suddenly there was Purcell again', as it was said when, out of Canterbury Cathedral, this sound returned to the world after centuries of misunderstanding and indifference. By this was meant that only the discovery and subsequent career of Alfred Deller enabled Purcell, once again, to be properly appreciated and understood.

There is nothing inappropriate in having switched from our imaginary picture of medieval monks slipping into their Quire, to Alfred Deller and the Second World War. In that war, as in the middle ages, the Cathedral in the winter months was cold and dark. Over and above these austerities, it was a target for the bombs. But still there were the regular services, twice daily, week by week; and Canterbury's Cathedral was never more truly the spiritual centre of the city's life. Canterbury during the war was so empty that one could go out into its main street and there would be only a few people about, and probably not a single motor vehicle in sight. Those who remained were bound together in a new intensity of living, which was like some peculiar and miraculous 'trip': unforgettable, unrepeatable. Precentor Joseph Poole, who was responsible for the Cathedral's music throughout those years, expressed it afterwards by saying: 'Being on the brink of eternity made it so much more fun to be here.' That was one aspect of the truth. The other aspect was an experience of recurring dread, which was not fun and did not even remind one of eternity but simply of death.

A few weeks after VE day, when the choir which had been trained single-handedly by Joseph Poole gave a lunch-hour recital at the National Gallery in London, it was spoken of by critics as being the finest Cathedral choir in England at that time. That this could have been so seems little short of miraculous. At the outset of the war, the Choir School with its headmaster had rightly been evacuated to Cornwall, while the organist, who was normally responsible for their training, was conscripted into the R.A.F. From twenty-four boarders and the same number of day boys, there remained in Canterbury half a dozen small boys, together with five adult lay-clerks. (Among the latter was Alfred Deller who, as a conscientious objector, remained at the Cathedral throughout the war, while working as a stretcher bearer at the hospital, and on a local farm.) It was providential for the Cathedral to have in its Precentor an outstanding musician, who took this apparently unpromising nucleus and built up from it, in the most difficult circumstances, the founda-

tion of the Cathedral's post-war music. If credit has not always
been given where credit is most due, this is perhaps not inappropriate. Although there is no basis for the legend that the great
artists of our medieval Cathedrals were invariably anonymous, it is
at least true that they cared nothing for the perpetuation of their
own names, but only for the work.

Incised upon the weathered stone of a buttress at the east end of
the Cathedral is a fifteenth century epitaph. The Latin must have
been translated at a time when it was easier to read than it is at
present: *Here lies Humbert on whom God have mercy. May he live with
Christ now that he has been withdrawn from this world. In his mouth
were the praises of God in the evening and in the morning of the day. That
of which he sang so well in life hath death revealed to him.*

AN ACCOUNT of the burning down of Ernulf's Quire and its rebuilding by William of Sens has been left us by a monk of the Priory

named Gervase, who was an eye-witness of these events.[1] On September the ninth in the year 1174 there was a high wind. A fire broke out among the cottages in Burgate Street and caused some excitement. When this was extinguished, the citizens went home without having noticed that a few sparks and cinders had been blown across to the roof of the Cathedral and were smouldering merrily amongst the rafters and beams, concealed by the vaulting below and the sheet-lead covering above. It was some hours before someone observed that flames were beginning to shoot out.

Then the people and the monks assemble in haste, they draw water, they brandish their hatchets, they run up the stairs, full of eagerness to save the church, already, alas! beyond their help. But when they reach the roof and perceive the black smoke and scorching flames that pervade it throughout, they abandon the attempt in despair, and thinking only of their own safety, make all haste to descend.

And now that the fire had loosened the beams from the pegs that bound them together, the half-burnt timbers fell into the choir below upon the seats of the monks; the seats, consisting of a great mass of wood-work caught fire, and thus this mischief grew worse and worse. And it was marvellous, though sad, to behold how that glorious choir itself fed and assisted the fire that was destroying it. For the flames multiplied by this mass of timber, and extending upwards full fifteen cubits, scorched and burnt the walls, and more especially injured the columns of the church.

And now the people ran to the ornaments of the church, and began to tear down the pallia and curtains, some that they might save, but some to steal them. The reliquary chests were thrown down from the high beam and thus broken, and their contents scattered; but the monks collected them and carefully preserved them from the fire. Some there were, who, inflamed with a wicked and diabolical cupidity, feared not to appropriate to themselves the things of the church, which they had saved from the fire.

In this manner the house of God, hitherto delightful as a paradise of pleasures, was now made a despicable heap of ashes, reduced to a dreary wilderness, and laid open to all injuries of the weather.

The people were astonished that the Almighty should suffer such things, and maddened with excess of grief and perplexity, they tore their hair and beat the walls and pavement of the church with their heads and hands, blaspheming the Lord and His saints, the patrons of the church; and many both of laity and monks, would rather have laid down their lives than that the church should have so miserably perished.

Gervase, writing many years later, seems positively to revel in past anguish, reflecting perhaps that good was eventually to come out of it. His description of the lamentations of the bereaved monks recalls to us an age when emotions were more simply and uninhibitedly expressed.

[1] The quotations following are from the translation given by the Rev. Robert Willis M.A., F.R.S. in *Architectural History of Some English Cathedrals. Part 1*. Paul P. B. Minet. Chicheley. 1972.

Truly that they might alleviate their miseries with a little consolation, they put together as well as they could, an altar and station in the nave of the church, where they might wail and howl rather than sing the diurnal and nocturnal services. Meanwhile the patron saints of the church, St. Dunstan and St. Elphege, had their resting place in that wilderness. Lest, therefore, they should suffer even the slightest injury from the rains and storms, the monks, weeping and lamenting with incredible grief and anguish, opened the tombs of the saints and extricated them in their coffins from the choir, but with the greatest difficulty and labour, as if the saints themselves resisted the change.

(The body of St. Thomas, by the way, did not have to suffer all this shifting about: it was, at this time, buried safely in the Crypt.)

The Community resigned itself temporarily to occupying the east end of the Nave. That winter they must have been colder than ever, as the draughts whistled through whatever boarding they had temporarily erected between themselves and the open ruins beyond. Those ruins would have constantly reminded them of what had once been the pride of their hearts. Some of them could even remember the time when that marvellous Quire was being built. Old men, thinking back to their boyhood, would ramble on to their younger brethren of the artists and craftsmen who had covered its walls and ceilings with the glorious paintings which had vanished, almost all of them, overnight.

Eventually they pulled themselves together and set about looking for an architect. Some of those they consulted (and the fact that 'French and English artificers were summoned' as a matter of course, reminds us that in those days there was a channel tunnel in men's minds, a constant to-ing and fro-ing between here and the continent) pretended to be able to repair the whole without damage to what was left; others said frankly that the whole of that part of the church must be pulled down and entirely rebuilt: 'This opinion, true as it was, excruciated the monks with grief. . . .'

However, amongst the other workmen there had come a certain William of Sens, a man active and ready, and as a workman most skilful both in wood and stone. Him, therefore, they retained, on account of his lively genius and good reputation, and dismissed the others. And to him, and to the providence of God was the execution of the work committed.

And he, residing many days with the monks and carefully surveying the burnt walls in their upper and lower parts, within and without, did yet for some time conceal what he found necessary to be done, lest the truth should kill them in their present state of pusillanimity.

But he went on preparing all things that were needful for the work. . . .

William seems to have been a wonderfully tactful and diplomatic man. He waited until the monks were 'somewhat comforted' and then confessed to them that a very great deal of the ruin must be destroyed if the building was to be made safe. Even so, he was prepared to compromise and contrive. He promised to retain the two chapels of St. Andrew and St. Anselm to the east of the Quire; and even to work into his designs the remnants of the walls of the two Quire aisles, although this must have presented him with problems which would have baffled a lesser architect beyond the limits of his patience. Altogether he must have been a positive Leonardo of a man. He not only produced the designs and took part in the work but 'constructed ingenious machines for loading and unloading ships and for drawing cement and stones . . . and other things of the same kind'. The Quire was pulled down 'and nothing else was done in this year'.

In the detailed description which follows there is a ring of the opening chapters of the Old Testament. Gervase gives us a blow-by-blow account of what was done, almost as if he were seeing Master William in the role of the Almighty creating the heavens and the earth. He tells us that in the second year, before the winter, there were erected four pillars, and after the winter two more, and so on until the September of the year 1178: 'All which things appeared to us and to all who saw them, incomparable and most worthy of praise.' The columns of William's Quire are alternately circular and octagonal, their capitals formed of curling fronds carved with consummate skill, in some cases, we may suppose, by the hand of the Master himself. What strikes us with amazement, as we examine the details of the work, is the perfection of its harmony with what remains from the previous building, although the two styles are so different. In the south quire aisle one sees where a portion of the norman arcading must have been impossible to preserve, and William has replaced it by a small pointed arch, delicately chiselled in the new style, an 'odd man out' which somehow looks delightfully 'right'. We see, too, how in the aisles and transepts an extraordinary conversion has taken place, too complex for the layman to understand although he may fully appreciate the harmony of the result, whereby the viable remains of the norman building have been preserved and incorporated into the work. All this has been achieved without a suggestion of uneasiness on account of the massive technical problems which must have been involved: there is a kind of simplicity and playfulness in the overall effect. Finally, there is the secretive playfulness of children in the three tiny faces among the acanthus leaves, high up on one of the purbeck marble shafts, on

The insouciance of William
of Sens. Mixed Norman
and Transitional arcading
in the South Quire aisle.

the south side. The one facing to the north-east is said to be a self-portrait carved by William himself. The other two are inhuman: one of them is actually an animal, while the other appears to be the ubiquitous Green Man with his mouthful of leaves. The most minute examination of the remaining capitals reveals no further interference with the formal grandeur of their curling fronds. Only this scarcely visible trinity – the man, the beast and the oddity in-between – seems to be making gentle fun, up there, all by itself.

One assumes that William must have sketched out designs for the completed work. These would have included the new Trinity Chapel east of the Quire, which was destined to be the place of the Shrine; for the Community had already been making plans for the removal of the sacred remains from the Crypt to a resting place at once more honourable and more convenient. For William, however, there was to be an end to all plans. On September 13th 1178 between twelve and two o'clock there was a partial eclipse:

> For the body of the sun appeared horned, with the horns turned west-ward, like the moon when she is twenty days old. The remainder of the

sun's circumference was not to be seen. For a certain black sphere
covered the splendour of the sun, and gradually descending, caused the
horned brightness to revolve around its upper part, until its points hung
down and looked towards the earth. But as that black thing slowly
pursued its course, these horns which were first turned to the west now
pointed to the east, as in the new moon. And then the black sphere passed
away, and the sun resumed his brightness.

This display, which sounds like a TV space-fiction programme
lacking only the electronic accompaniment, had a sobering effect
upon the monks. Something, they felt, was going to happen. A few
days later, Master William was up in the scaffolding 'in the act of
preparing the machines for the turning of the great vault', when
suddenly the wooden scaffolding gave way and he fell from a height
of fifty feet. Gervase seems to be undecided as to which of the two
major supernatural agencies was at work: 'Thus sorely bruised by
the blows from the beams and stones, he was rendered helpless alike
to himself and for the work, but no other person than himself was in
the least injured. Against the master only was the vengeance of God
or spite of the devil directed.'

William retired to his bed; but 'his health amended not'. Winter
approached and it was necessary to complete the vault; so the
master entrusted the work 'to a certain ingenious and industrious
monk, who was the overseer of the masons, an appointment whence
much envy and malice arose, because it made this young man
appear more skilful than richer and more powerful ones. But the
master reclining in bed commanded all things that should be done
in order.' Time seems to fold up and slide away as we picture it:

the bickering, the angry complaints, the tired pain-racked man, desperately fighting to continue his work. Of course it would not do.

'And the master, perceiving that he derived no benefit from the physicians, gave up the work and, crossing the sea, returned to his home in France.'

Opposite
Bell Harry Tower in 1816, seen from what is now the Archbishop's garden, across the west wall of the Cloister.

One of the two clusters of foliage, facing one another at the crossing of the Quire, tucked into the arcading of Prior Eastry's lateral screens.

THE MONKS put the work of rebuilding into the hands of another William. Gervase describes him as being 'small in body but in workmanship of many kinds acute and honest'. It has become customary to speak of him as William the Englishman for the purpose of distinguishing his work from that of William of Sens. The Frenchman had completed the Quire, as far as the fifth row of columns extending east from the crossing (traditionally the site of his accident). One assumes that he left plans for the rest; but his successor, being a Master in his own right, would have allowed himself plenty of scope. His, then, is the place of the Shrine, the Trinity Chapel with its semi-

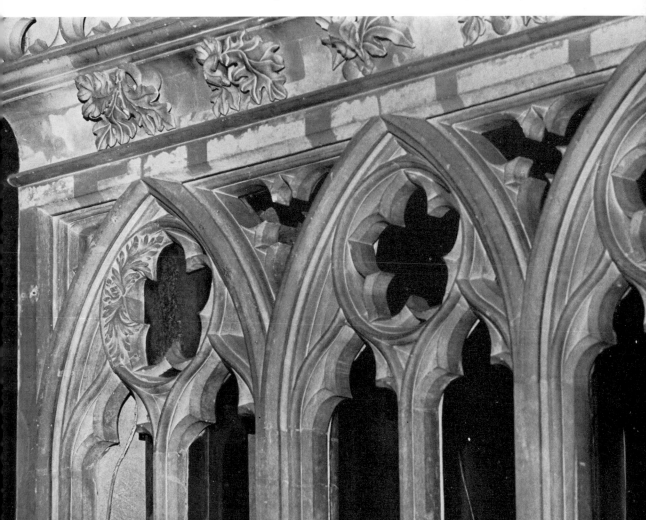

circular ambulatory, opening up behind the High Altar in graceful magnificence. Beneath this he designed and supervised the building of the Eastern Crypt. The Western Crypt was undamaged by the fire: it is now the oldest part of the Cathedral and is generally referred to as 'Ernulf's Crypt'.

The High Altar of the Quire stands now at the top of a tremendous flight of steps. The communion rail, considerably below it, extends across a wide platform which was the original site of the altar it-self. The ancient marble seat of the Archbishop, now in the Corona, stood then where the altar stands now, to the west of the shrine. The present arrangement focuses the eyes upon the highest level of the Church, the point at which the presbytery is nipped in to its narrowest extent. There is something aesthetically satisfying about this; but still one cannot wholeheartedly agree with a policy which goes against the sacred geometry according to which the Gothic cathedrals are known to have been built. We no longer understand this geometry, but we know that the position of the High Altar was an essential key to it.[1]

On either side, above the seating in the Quire, run Prior Eastry's screens. These are described with inimitable economy in Warner's excellent text book[2] as 'a series of double lights under a moulded arch with a five-cusped circle in the head, the whole surmounted by a cornice enriched with foliage, trefoils and battlements'. The Grand Old Man had them erected at some time during his long priorate, probably early in the fourteenth century, and they stand as his chief memorial, his greatest work. To the west they are hidden from the Quire by the imposing Return Stalls erected in 1682; on the other side, from the Nave, by Chillenden's[3] more elaborate screen; but as one passes through the entrance at the top of the Nave steps, one can see and feel the older screen on either hand, and lay one's palm against the indentation made by the swinging of the aspersorium or holy water sprinkler on its long chain. One of the incidental charms of Eastry's screen is the spray of sculptured foliage which occurs twice only, in the two cusped circles nearest the transept gates.

Of the three entrances to the Quire, the one to the north is con-temporaneous with the screen; while that to the south, being a little later (*circa* 1340), is delightful in presenting us with the only ball flower ornament to be found in the Cathedral. Beyond it, our eyes are smitten by a positive tornado of coloured glass. The modern windows by the Hungarian artist Bossanyi, inserted in the south-east transept shortly after the Second World War, are inappro-

Opposite, top right
Traces of what must once have been radiant suns in the South Quire aisle below the arcading of Prior Eastry's screen.

Opposite, bottom right
The only example of ball flower ornament in the Cathedral decorates the south doorway of the Quire.

[1] As this book goes to press, there are plans to remove the altar to its original site.
[2] *Canterbury Cathedral*. S. A. Warner. SPCK. 1923.
[3] The present pulpitum is known generally by this name; although recent scholarship has produced a theory that not only the figures of the six kings but the screen itself is mid-15th century in date. It is not within the scope of this book or the competence of its author to discuss these finer points.

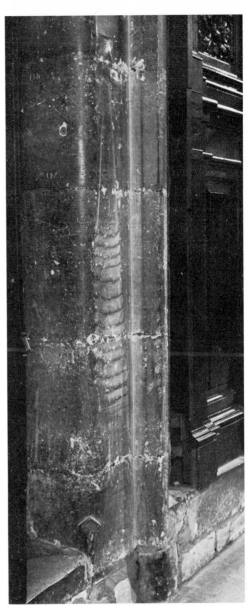

priate in colour to the whole character of the Cathedral and even more inappropriate in sentiment.

Opposite, high up in the north-east transept, is Canterbury's Rose Window, of which the central figures and some of those surrounding them are ancient. The former represent Moses and the Synagogue: the heads are restorations by George Austin. The window as a whole, while containing a set of fascinating twelfth century personifications of the Cardinal Virtues (Fortitude, in particular, is a lovely witch-like creature, holding a drawn sword with which she appears to be lashing vindictively at a coil of rope), exemplifies the

Above
'. . . the indentation made by the swinging of the *aspersorium* or holy water sprinkler.'

devotion and skill of the Victorian glaziers of the Cathedral work-shop. Two windows which were happily in no need of such treatment, gleam in the shadows of the north quire aisle, with a richness of pure colour unrivalled elsewhere in the building: all that remains of a series of twelve 'Bible' windows, which must have been placed in the aisles very shortly after the rebuilding by William of Sens. The object of these windows was the teaching of the Gospels, in such a way as to bring out certain correspondences with episodes from the Old Testament. They are also known as 'Type and Anti-type' windows. The Anti-types are the events in the life of Christ. The Types are the pre-figurations of those events. So we get a medallion of Lot's wife disobeying the warning against 'turning back', alongside one depicting the Three Kings (in bed with their crowns on) receiving a similar warning in their sleep. The east window of the Corona, partially restored, is of the same kind, extra to the series of twelve.

These windows, besides their glory of colour and excellence of design, exemplify to perfection that peculiar humour, childlike, yet faintly diabolical, like the fun-poking of some misshapen, not unkindly elf, which only the middle ages could produce. It is interesting to compare them with the painstaking and in many ways admirable Victorian imitations – of which there are still a few in the Cathedral, despite a deplorable tendency to replace them by pretentious and sentimental modern glass which is both less interesting and less aesthetically pleasant. Apart from the obvious inferiority of colour, the neo-medieval work produced during the last hundred years or so seems lifeless, unspontaneous, flat. What secret did those twelfth and thirteenth century craftsmen possess, whereby they imbued even figures designed in glass – above all, perhaps, figures designed in glass – with such vitality that they seem almost visibly to pulsate, without in any way denying the hardness and non-plasticity of the material with which they worked?

Above these windows and their equivalents (now filled in with ancient glass from a private collection, recently purchased) in the south quire aisle, are others of the same date which are visible only from the Quire itself. These depict, on the north side, legends of St. Alphege and St. Dunstan; on the south, scenes from the life of the Virgin Mary (the figures in this series being heavily restored). The roundel depicting the siege of Canterbury by the Danes is a marvel of economy in design; but the subjects, on the whole, are not easily made out without the use of binoculars: one has to be content with the overall jewel-like effect.

Eᴀꜱᴛ ᴏꜰ the crossing, a number of canopied archiepiscopal tombs break the progress of Prior Eastry's lateral screens. These tombs are best studied from the aisles. The first to arrest one's attention is that of Archbishop Henry Chichele to the north. This elaborate fifteenth century monument has been given more than its fair share of attention in comparison with those of the fourteenth century Archbishops Stratford and Simon of Sudbury on the opposite side. Stratford's tomb, in particular, is remarkable for the delicately sculptured arcading on the facade of the marble table on which the figure lies recumbent. Small creatures of doubtful identity decorate this elegantly finished piece of work. Similar but more sinister-looking creatures appear on the canopy of Sudbury's tomb, further east. Noses pointing downwards, wings folded on their backs, they are bat-like, faintly demonish. The remains of poor Simon Sudbury, interred beneath, consist of his decapitated body and a cannon ball to represent his head, which reposes in the churchyard of his native village in Suffolk. Scapegoat for the Establishment, he was clumsily beheaded by Wat Tyler's mob on Tower Hill.

Why then, with all this beauty and drama on the opposite side, is Chichele's tomb the most famous and, in the strictest sense of the word, remarkable of this particular little huddle of tombs? The answer seems to be that it is brightly coloured (having been heavily repainted and restored), extremely elaborate, inordinately high, and singled out by a rather startling feature which is typical of the late middle ages in their morbid preoccupation with death. Chichele ordered his tomb to be made during his lifetime. It is said that his choice of design was influenced by his feelings of remorse, on account of the encouragement he had given to the warlike activities of King Henry V. The Archbishop is represented by two figures: the one in full pontificals, mitred and robed, the hands uplifted in prayer, supported at the four corners by four angels; the other, beneath it, a naked cadaver reposing on a shroud. (It is curious that only the robed figure is shown as praying for and receiving supernatural assistance: the poor corpse, divested of all its temporal honours and possessions, appears to have been deserted by this world and the next.)

A comical but not altogether pleasant little story is related in connection with this monument. In the year 1425, a criminal sought sanctuary in the Cathedral. Pursued by a crowd of the righteous, he dived through the iron railings surrounding the tomb and crouched there, presumably in the ground-floor compartment with the naked corpse (with whose afflicted state he felt some

'. . . cleansed of all popery
he lies . . . in snow-white
marble on his back':
Archbishop Archibald
Campbell Tait.

affinity no doubt). The monks, who were celebrating High Mass in the Quire at the time, were much put out by the commotion, as the godly citizens belaboured the poor man with cudgels through the rails and endeavoured to seize him by the arms and legs. So unseemly was this episode in the opinion of the Prior that he demanded redress money on account of it. The civic authorities paid up.

Instructive as it may be to compare the two figures on Chichele's tomb, it is more amusing to compare the entire concept of that tomb with a monument, in its own way equally impressive, which lies across the way from it, in the north-east transept. Archbishop Archibald Campbell Tait, epitome of Victoriana, lies prone in snow-white marble on his back, clearly in confident expectation of being met by a committee of welcome at the heavenly gates. Not for him the ostentatious magnificence of the past. Cleansed of all popery he lies, the great puffed gathered-in sleeves of *Ecclesia Anglicana* displayed in all their dignity upon his breast. A small great-niece of this formidable prelate was nearly frightened out of her wits on being introduced to him suddenly by her nurse. 'That, dear', said Old Nan, her voice swelling with pride as she contemplated what was to her the Cathedral's premier shrine, 'is your great-uncle.' The appalled child, in expectation of the imminent arousal of Uncle Archie in

Details from the tomb of Archbishop Bourchier in the North Quire aisle.

response to this presentation, let out a howl and was promptly removed from the sacred precincts. It was an odd start for someone who was to pursue a love affair with Canterbury Cathedral throughout most of her life. 'Can you remember', her mother was to ask her years later, 'why you always used to cry when we went into Canterbury and say: "Not the big church, Mummy, *not* the big church!"'

Two other Archbishops are memorialised in the north-east transept. Of its two apsidal chapels, that to the south was restored after the Second World War in memory of Cosmo Gordon Lang (its pair on the opposite side of the Quire commemorates his successor, William Temple, in polished black and grey marbles of considerable beauty and a design of sweeping elegance). An outwardly imposing figure, solitary and unknowable in his personal life, Archbishop Lang was regarded in his lifetime and is remembered now as the personification of the Establishment: this 'image', however, does him less than justice. Lang was a staunch Conservative and an almost obsessive royalist; but it needs to be recalled that he was the firm friend of two disturbingly unconventional Deans. Dean Hewlett Johnson, the 'Red Dean', who presided at the consecration of three successive archbishops after Lang's retirement, would respond to the mention of his name with a reminiscent smile. 'Cosmo', he would say, 'was the one I liked best.' This simple statement is the best possible answer to the generally accepted notion that these two were the deadliest enemies on account of their political disagreements. Both men, after all, were great lovers of the Cathedral. Lang, in his old age, during the first summer of the war, was in the habit of emerging almost daily from the Palace simply to look at it and then go back. A frail figure, encased in black, he would toddle across the deserted Precincts and turn round, always on the same spot. There he would stand for several minutes, gazing steadily upwards at Bell Harry tower. Among all the countless pictures of the Cathedral which have slid away into that dimension which contains the past, is this of the old Archbishop, isolated in the summer sunshine, leaning back upon an ebony stick, staring and staring at beauty as if he could never have enough. He always wore white kid gloves.

The chapel to the north is associated with the name of Lanfranc. It seems probable that his remains still lie hidden somewhere in the vicinity of this altar, to which they were removed after the great fire of 1174. On the south wall is a very early scratching: the word

Opposite
In this nineteenth century print of the North Quire aisle, robed clergy and choir boys are seen waiting outside the vestry in St. Andrew's Chapel, as they often do today. The north entrance to the Quire is seen on the right. Beside it is Archbishop Chichele's tomb.

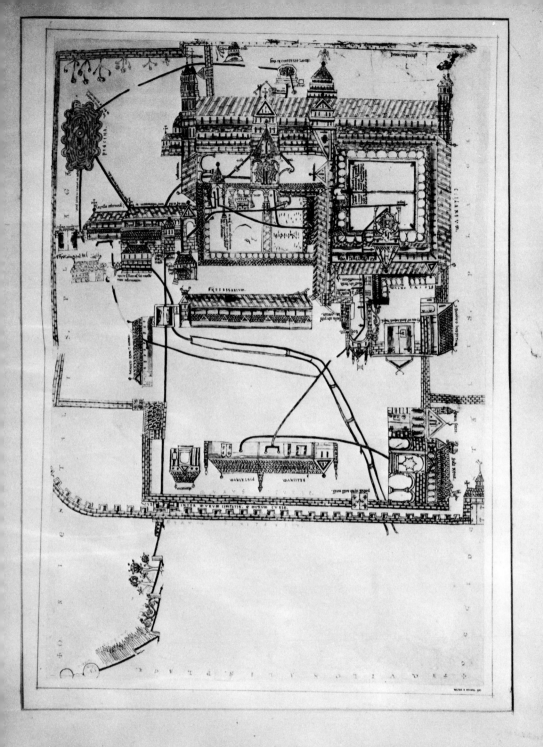

:PLAN OF PRIOR WIBERT'S WATER WORKS
circa 1160.
:DETAIL OF THE DISTRIBUTION IN RELATION TO
:THE CATHEDRAL AND ITS PRECINCTS.

:From a copy of the Utrecht Psalter made by Edwine, a monk of Christ Church, Canterbury,
:and reproduced by permission, from the original in the library of Trinity College, Cambridge.

Opposite
Eadwine's plan of Prior
Wibert's water system.
Note 1) The twin towers of
St. Andrew and St. Anselm
rising above their respective
chapels. 2) The Water
Tower adjoining the NE
transept. 3) The monastic
bathhouse against the
north alley of the
Cloisters. 4) The monastic
fishpond due east of the
Cathedral. 5) The seraph on
the Angel steeple.

'Lanfranc' and a beautiful little pentagram, one of the most ancient
and universal of magical signs. The pentagram drawn 'clockwise' is
a safeguard against evil influences from without, a sign of the in-
tegrity of the good. Drawn in the reverse direction it looks the same
but is believed to have an opposite effect. On the north wall is a
similar scratching which reads *Ediva Regina*, and refers to the Saxon
Queen of that name who lies buried in this apse. Ediva, as we are
reminded in the poem attached to her portrait (a fifteenth century
painting on wood) was the mother of three Saxon Kings. She was
also the friend of the saintly Archbishop Odo, on whose account she
presented the Cathedral with gifts of land to assist with repairs to
the roof. Of these repairs Eadmer writes:

But because it was absolutely necessary that the Divine Service should
not be interrupted, and no temple could be found sufficiently capacious
to receive the multitude of the people, the archbishop prayed to heaven
that until the work should be completed, neither rain nor wind might be
suffered to intrude within the walls of the Church, so as to prevent the
performance of the service. And so it came to pass: for during three years
in which the walls of the Church were being carried upwards, the whole
building remained open to the sky: yet did no rain fall either within the
walls of the Church, or even within the walls of the City, that could
impede the clergy standing in the Church in the performance of their duty,
or restrain the people from coming even to the beginning of it. And truly
it was a sight worth seeing, to behold the space beyond the walls of the
city drenched with water, while the walls themselves remained perfectly
dry.

Piercing the north wall of the transept are four narrow slits.
These are peepholes, made about the year 1500 for the use of the
Prior, so that he might join in the services from the privacy of his own
chapel and occasionally, one assumes, keep a wary eye upon his
monks. The Prior's chapel was situated on the other side of the wall.
The gracefully arched doorway which used to lead into it is mid-
thirteenth century in date; and may still be seen on the right-hand
side of the passage from the north transept to the upper storey of the
Water Tower, the communal wash-house. The explanation of this
delectable little octagonal tower (this upper part of which was rebuilt in the time of Prior Chillenden) is contained in a print which
hangs on the wall to the left. This depicts Eadwine's plan of the
monastic waterworks. In the mid-twelfth century Prior Wibert
installed an elaborate and, for those days, positively sensational
hydraulic system for the use of the monks. From springs of pure
water issuing from ground to the north-east of the Cathedral, he
ordered the laying of pipes to a circular conduit house and thence

to the city wall, across the moat by a bridge, and so into the Cathedral precincts. On its way the water passed through five settling-tanks. Once safely in the precincts it was carried round in a manner which appears on the plan like the windings and coilings of a rope. The Water Tower itself had a central pillar through which the water was conveyed to a basin in the upper room. The passageway (already described) between this room and the north-east transept was used by the monks when they came from their Dormitory to the Cathedral, pausing on the way for a cold and perfunctory splash. It was due to the efficiency of this system that the dreaded epidemics which swept across Europe in the middle ages, including the Black Death, passed lightly over the Priory of Christ Church. Prior Wibert was responsible for a number of buildings within the monastic precincts, including the Aula Nova or North Hall, which was later used to house the poorer pilgrims to the Shrine of St. Thomas. He must have been a man of exceptional practical ability and intelligence.

The Cathedral itself is said (almost incredibly) to be founded on a bog. In the eighteen-thirties when the north-west tower was demolished, workmen came upon the upright skeletons of a man and two oxen, relics of a pre-historic tragedy in the engulfing swamp. And in 1888, when a deep trench was being dug in the Eastern Crypt, the workmen were splashing in water, prompting one of the Canons to remark that 'wherever one dug one came to the bog on which the Cathedral was built'.[1]

Opposite
Prior Wibert's Water Tower, the upper part of which was rebuilt in the early fifteenth century under the auspices of Prior Chillenden.

[1] Quoted in *What became of the Bones of Becket?* by A. J. Mason (1920).

THE TWO norman chapels of St. Andrew and St. Anselm, on either side of the Quire, were carefully preserved by William of Sens. His successor, the Englishman, presumably in accordance with designs already laid down, made room for them by nipping in the new Quire sharply to the east. The result is, like so many other oddities in the Cathedral, entirely satisfying and right. The Quire moves forwards and upwards to a narrowed-in point (which has the effect of making it seem very much longer, even, than it actually is), beyond which there is a sudden blossoming out. Without this narrowing there would have been, on either side, insufficient space between chapel and screen to accommodate the steps leading upwards to the place of the Shrine.

The two chapels are pure romanesque. That of St. Andrew to the north is used as the vestry. Dividing it from the quire aisle is a portion

of Prior Eastry's screen, removed from the eastern extension of the Quire to accommodate Archbishop Howley's monument. Somewhere near the site of this monument there was, in medieval times, an enormous chest containing relics. It is worth a moment's pause to consider a few of the startling objects which were housed in this chest and taken out, for a suitable consideration in each case, to be contemplated and kissed. For instance:

Aaron's rod.
A piece of the clay out of which the Lord made Adam.
Part of the oak upon which someone (described in the inventory as Abraham) climbed to see the Lord.
A piece of woollen material woven by Our Lady.
A piece of the prison from which Peter was rescued by the Angel.
A piece of the table of the Last Supper.
Three heads (St. Blaise, St. Furse and St. Austroberta).
Eleven arms.
Masses of assorted bones.
A surprising number of portions of the True Cross.
And a great deal else, including of course innumerable relics of St. Thomas.

But all this is by the way. The chapel of St. Anselm, on the south side, has a charisma of its own, a tenderness of sanctity preserved within the formula of its great beauty but deriving, one assumes, essentially from the influence of the saint. The body of St. Anselm was laid to rest beneath the pavement of this chapel: whether or not it is still there we do not know (King Henry VIII is said to have ordered the destruction of all the shrines in the Cathedral, without necessarily in all cases disturbing the bones) but there is no doubt whatsoever of his continuing presence. If ever there was a true saint in Canterbury St. Anselm was that saint. His biography by the monk Eadmer[1] has qualities of sincerity and credibility not often to be found in medieval hagiographies of this sort. Anselm was appointed to Canterbury from the abbacy of Bec. He shrank from high office, being far better suited to the contemplative life and scholastic pursuits. Throughout his primacy he was beset with troubles. Devoted as he became to the Cathedral and its family of monks, he was constantly being torn away from them by practical affairs, and a considerable part of his sixteen years as Primate were spent in exile on the continent. Like Becket, he quarrelled with his King; but he had more excuse: William Rufus was not a particularly amiable individual by all accounts. When the arrow dispatched him unprepared, his good Archbishop (to the pardonable surprise of the

An old print showing the Chapel of St. Anselm from the South Quire aisle, workmen making themselves pleasantly at home in a shaft of sunlight.

[1] *The Life of St. Anselm.* Eadmer. Ed. and trans. by R. W. Southern. Clarendon Press. Oxford. 1962.

onlookers) burst into tears and declared that he would rather have died himself than that the King should do so in his present state.

Anselm appears to have been a psychic sensitive as well as a saint: presumably his religious exercises developed in him unusual powers; in any case the 'miraculous' stories related of him by Eadmer are mostly entirely credible, having to do with clairvoyance and the healing of the sick. Like every other Archbishop of Canterbury up to the time of the Dissolution, he was the titular Abbot of the Christ Church monks; and Eadmer, as one of those monks, is at pains to impress upon the reader the truly fatherly nature of the relationship in this case. On one occasion, we are told, when Anselm was presiding at a meeting of the Chapter, he smiled and said: 'Just as an owl is glad when she is in her hole with her chicks and (in her fashion) all is well with her; and just as she is attacked and torn to pieces when she is among crows and rooks and other birds, and everything then is far from well with her, so it is with me. For when I am with you, all is well with me, and this is the joy and consolation of my life. But when I am separated from you, and my ways lie among men who are in the world' — by this time the old man had ceased to smile and was weeping bitterly — 'then I am torn this way and that. . . .'

We can imagine him mixing freely with the monks, engaging them in hair-splitting theological arguments. Eadmer tells us that whenever they grew worried that the pressure of secular affairs was affecting his health, they would take him aside and craftily put to him some question of scriptural exegesis, luring him tenderly into a metaphysical dispute. Intellectually and spiritually he was a giant. But his sanctity was Franciscan in type. On one occasion 'while he was hastening to his manor at Hayes, the boys of his household with their dogs chased a hare which they came upon in the road. As they were pursuing it, it fled beneath the feet of the horse on which Anselm sat. The horse stood still; and Anselm — knowing that the wretched animal looked to find a place of refuge beneath him and not wishing to deny it the help it needed — drew his horse by the reins and kept it still. The dogs came round, snuffing about on all sides and restrained against their will, but they could neither make it move from under the horse, nor harm it in any way. We were astonished at the sight. But Anselm, when he saw some of the horsemen laugh and make merry at the expense of the cornered animal, burst into tears and said: "You laugh, do you? But there is no laughing, no merry making, for this unhappy beast. His enemies stand round about him, and in fear of his life he flies to us asking

Opposite
Interior of the same chapel *circa* 1950. The workmen are still around but the post-war redecorators are yet to come.

for help." ' At this point he introduced a comparison between the bewildered animal and the soul in the moment of death. Then he raised his voice and forbade the dogs to approach. They obeyed him, as all creatures are accustomed to obeying the saints. The hare leapt up unhurt and fled into the woods.

Many are the tales of compassion which Eadmer relates. No wonder that when the Archbishop was dead and his body was buried in the very chapel where we now recall him, it was said that a flowery fragrance drifted in the air about his tomb. He died on Palm Sunday in the year 1109 at the age of seventy-six. Just before he died one of the Brothers had been reading to him from the gospel of the day. As he began to breathe more slowly, they lifted him gently from his bed and laid him, as was customary, on sackcloth and ashes on the ground. Every Christian in the middle ages prayed fervently for a good death. Anselm received an answer to his prayer. 'The whole congregation of his sons gathered round him, and sending forth his soul into the hands of the Creator, he slept in peace.'

Eadmer admits disarmingly that in writing the biography of his beloved Father, he 'was not free from the sin of disobedience'. Anselm had discovered him in the act and ordered him to destroy what he had written. Eadmer did so, but not before he had made a copy of it, which he then finished. Therefore he asks that whoever reads his book shall pray for his sin to be forgiven. One wonders how many actually do so. And yet it is a heartfelt request; and in the chapel of St. Anselm Eadmer too is almost tangibly present. Nothing can really spoil this chapel; although it must be said that various well-intentioned persons seem to have done their best. Originally it was painted all over in pure bright colours, an example of this scheme being visible still, high up in the north-east corner: a painting of St. Paul and the serpent, preserved through the centuries by the chance of some walling having been at some time built across it to cover it up. Some people may prefer the austere beauty of the unpainted stone; but there is no denying the brilliant craftsmanship of this wonderfully decorative piece of work. Nor is there any reason why modern craftsmen, working in a contemporary idiom, should not do as well. Unfortunately the chapel received lavish attentions immediately after the Second World War, when religious sentimentality, cloaked beneath an exciting appearance of modernity, had fallen to the lowest depth it is ever likely to reach. The sinuous Calvary figures on the altar are typical of this period. So is the glass which now fills the great Decorated window in the south wall. One cannot but assume that the artist who was

Opposite
The Pilgrims' steps leading from the South Quire aisle to the place of the shrine.

responsible for this window was a migraine subject: he has certainly been eminently successful in producing a visual representation of an acute attack.

Eastwards from St. Anselm's are the Pilgrims' steps. Worn with the tramplings of great multitudes they go up to the place of the Shrine, the centre of the healing powers associated with the name of St. Thomas of Canterbury in the heyday of his cult.

'On the day of the festival', as a contemporary chronicler relates, 'wine ran freely through the gutters of the streets.' It was July 7 in the year 1220, the day of the Translation of St. Thomas, when the precious remains were translated from the tomb in the Crypt to the Trinity Chapel above.

The body of St. Thomas had been hastily buried in the Eastern Crypt, behind the altar of the Undercroft. It is thought that he himself had been responsible for the ordering of his own tomb. There it had remained for fifty years; even the fire of 1174 and the subsequent rebuilding of the Eastern Crypt by William the Englishman had not disturbed it: the monks had erected around it some sort of wall, and the pilgrims had continued to visit it as best they could. The one occasion on which the body may possibly have been removed was during the exile of the entire Community to France during the reign of King John. The walling-in of St. Gabriel's chapel, whereby its superb wall-paintings have been preserved to this day, may have been for the purpose of providing a hiding place for these and other relics during the absence of the monks.[1]

By the year 1220 the cult of St. Thomas was not only established but nearing its zenith. It had come into being almost overnight. This phenomenon has never been adequately explained. The explanation generally put forward, to the effect that it was expedient for Rome to encourage devotion to a martyr who had died for the rights of the Church over those of the State, seems irrelevant to so colossal an intoxication of the collective unconscious as actually took place. Canterbury was the Lourdes of those times. The water of St. Thomas' well,[2] tinted the palest pink to simulate the blood said to have been introduced into it from the moppings of the bloodied pavement, was the medicine of Christendom; while every conceivable object that had been (or was said to have been) touched by the saint had miraculous powers. So it was commonly believed; and so therefore, to a great extent, it actually was. The miracles are

[1] But see pg. 135
[2] Generally believed to have been the one in the infirmary cloisters close to the Water Tower.

exceptionally well documented. Not only were a great many of them recorded at the time; but the names of at least the local personalities involved have been traced. Among the first to be honoured by a manifestation was one Godefrid the Baker, whose child was apparently dead, when he got hold of a bloodstained rag — there seem to have been an astonishing number of bloodstained rags, but then after all (poor Thomas) why not? — and, soaking it in water, forced the resulting potion down the child's throat with excellent results. The story is the more convincing perhaps, in that Godefrid was not always on good terms with the Christ Church monks. A few years later, in the course of one of their perennial rows with successive archbishops, Gervase describes him as 'that son of Beliel', on account of his having taken sides against them along with William the Watchman and John the Cook.

The most spectacular of all the Canterbury pilgrims was King Henry himself. The treatment meted out to the monarch, who was not after all directly to blame, is typical of the medieval delight in situations of dramatic catharsis. Henry came to Canterbury in the summer of 1174. Dismounting from his horse about half a mile from the West Gate, he stripped off his clothes down to his woollen undershirt, and walked barefoot to the Cathedral down the main street. The story has been told so often that one loses the tang of it: the King himself, the crowned anointed King, walking the gauntlet of the gaping, pop-eyed citizens, head bowed and wearing nothing but a shirt beneath his cloak. This was only the beginning. Arriving at the Cathedral, he knelt first in the south-west porch; and then, going to the Martyrdom, bent down and kissed the hallowed pavement. One wonders what he was thinking. Did he remember his boon companion, his Thomas, and curse the impulse which had prompted him to make him archbishop? From the porch he went on to the Crypt. Kneeling before the tomb, he stripped to the waist and received five strokes with a rod from every bishop and abbot who was present, three from each one of the monks. His night was spent fasting in the Crypt. The next day he had a fever; but within the week his enemies by sea and land had been summarily dealt with by the saint.

Two more Kings had come and gone, and the young Henry III was on the throne, when the time came for the greatest celebration to have been held in the Cathedral since the body of St. Alphege had been received there in the presence of King Canute. The date of the Translation of St. Thomas of Canterbury was afterwards to be inscribed in the Calendar of the Church as a universal feast. One wonders if they deliberately timed it to be as close as possible to the summer solstice, allowing for the convenience of so many distinguished guests. One wonders if the day was fine and the sun shone on the gilded seraph on the central tower (the Angel steeple, they called it; Lanfranc's steeple; and the Angel had six wings, *with twain he covered his face and with twain his feet and with twain he did fly*). They were all of them there: Archbishop Stephen Langton, the thirteen-year-old King, all the bishops of the province, the Lord High Justiciary of England, the Archbishop of Rheims: so many important personages, the Lord Prior must have been hard put to it indeed to provide for them all appropriate entertainment. However, a considerable part of the financial burden on this occasion was incurred by the Archbishop. It was he who was said to have poured wine into the streets. The offerings at the Shrine amounted to something like (very roughly) £150,000, according to the value of money in 1976; and still the see of Canterbury was in debt for more than fifty years after the event. The French Archbishop celebrated Mass.

The Shrine of St. Thomas of Canterbury has been described in various ways, since we do not possess an exact representation of it. It appears to have been a 'gilded ark' encrusted with gems and supported on a marble base. The latter had arched openings to enable the pilgrims to grope within and touch with their fingers' ends the outer coffin of the saint. The jewels adorning the casket were of almost unbelievable magnificence. Important pilgrims vied with one another in the beauty and costliness of their offerings, most of which were simply fastened to the Shrine like so many barnacles, so that when at last they were carted away to the coffers of King Henry VIII, they 'filled two great chests such as six or seven strong men could doe no more than convey one of them out of the church'. Most spectacular of them all was the great ruby, the size of a hen's egg, known as the 'Regale' of France. The Regale was said to have leaped miraculously from the ring of King Louis VII and attached itself to the tomb in the Crypt. This episode took place when the poor King, in prayer before the tomb, turned a deaf ear to the Prior's repeated hints that he should present the ruby himself.

So they came . . . and came . . . and came. The strip cartoons of the great Miracle Windows overlooking the Shrine testified, as they do still, to the cures which were effected by the intercession, indeed by the active intervention in many cases, of the martyr-saint. Some of the pictures must have seemed distressingly frank to Victorian, Edwardian and Georgian tastes. As one Canon of the Cathedral recently remarked, while conducting a party of earnest-looking

'. . . a mist seems to come down and linger for a very long time.' This eighteenth century print of the Trinity Chapel reminds us of the long dreamy years when nothing in particular seemed to happen, while men and women continued to live out their lives in and around the Cathedral.

middle-aged ladies past a window depicting the miraculous restoration of somebody's amputated leg: 'St. Thomas seems to have been particularly fond of sticking things on after they'd been chopped off'.

But it was not only a question of miracles, of course.

Then longen folk to go on pilgrimage
And specially from every shire's end
Of England to Canterbury they wend
The holy blissful martyr for to seek.

A wonderful holiday, in the springtime before the weather got too hot, with free board and lodging at the Prior's expense.

What a fearful noise they must have made. One thinks of this now, when the noise made by the swarming tourists, throughout the long season, is so great that even the audio-system, relaying prayers at intervals with all its might, is defeated by it. But they came to pray, those pilgrims. And, exploited for their money as undoubtedly they were, the spiritual nourishment they received was more substantial than a few relayed prayers; it assaulted their eyes and their ears, it demanded to be received, it was everywhere they looked.

They were taken first to the Martyrdom transept, to the 'Altar of the Sword's Point'. This altar had been erected to mark the spot where Becket fell. It was made of wood. On it, probably in a glass-fronted jewelled reliquary, was the point of Le Breton's sword, growing rustier and more worn as the centuries passed. This was considered to be an exceptionally precious relic. Another was the hair shirt which hung over the original site of the tomb in the Crypt. The monks had been deeply impressed, when they came to remove the outer garments of the dead man, to discover this shirt — positively pullulating with vermin, if we may credit their gloating description of its edifying appearance. Another prized object was the hacked-off crown of St. Thomas's head: the *Caput Sancti Thome* as they called it, enclosed in a glittering reliquary and kept in the odd little chapel called the Corona at the extreme eastern end of the church. To all these holy places the pilgrims would be conducted by the monks. If one of them produced enough money or was sufficiently important, the reliquaries would be opened, the shirt taken down, and one after another the precious objects would be held out for him to kiss. Erasmus and Colet, visiting the Cathedral in the year 1513, when the cult was on the wane and the new humanism was spreading across Europe, were unenthusiastic at the prospect of physical contact with what appeared to be a very dirty old pocket-handkerchief. But Erasmus and Colet were late-comers to the scene; their reactions were a sign of the times. From the twelfth century onwards into the fifteenth, no monarch in Christendom would have slighted such an object; neither for that matter would he have been even momentarily repelled by it.

On their way to the Shrine itself the trooping pilgrims, their medieval minds forever playing with metaphor and image, must have felt as if they were mounting to the heavens up so many steps. Today this is the barest place in the Cathedral. It is kept so deliberately, of course. There is a cool, swept feeling about it. Not so for them. The great Shrine rose in all its splendour, covered at first by a gaudily painted canopy made of wood; before it was the altar of St. Thomas, gorgeously bedecked with jewelled cross and candlesticks: between this and the gleaming mandala of the *Opus Alexandrinum*, the intricate mosaic pavement, the pilgrims knelt. Awed and wondering, they queued for this moment. Those who were

Opposite
View from the place of the shrine, across the Opus Alexandrinum and down the Quire to the Nave.

grievously sick (we are thinking now of the poorer pilgrims; the rich and influential would come separately and be given exceptional privileges, regardless of their state of health) were permitted to approach more closely and reach between the arches of the lower part of the Shrine: one can imagine them scrabbling on the ground, weeping and crying out. *Thomas, Thomas, blessed Thomas, heal me . . . see, I am blind . . . see, I have a broken arm, I can no longer work . . . see, my little boy. . . .* The monks were so used to it all and to shifting them on. As for the multitudinous infections, the flaking scabs, the weeping sores, the noxious smells: within reason — unless it were leprosy or the plague — one took no notice. One lived in communion with such things, as one lived in communion with the beauty of nature and the beauty of human art, from morning till night.

But one did not live from morning till night in such a place as this. When all was in readiness the canopy would be raised by ropes attached to a pulley high up in the vault. A clamour of tinkling sound, from a fringe of silver bells, would proclaim the unveiling of the treasure trove beneath. Never had there been such a sight. The Shrine was plated with gold; against this was an intricate design in gold wire twisted into loops: affixed to this background were the clustering gems — diamonds and sapphires, rubies, emeralds and pearls, balasses, agates, cornelians, beryls, onyx stones: nothing that the riches and power of men were able to obtain had been left out. The gilded figure of an angel pointed an arresting finger at the great Regale. This had become an object almost of religious awe. It was said to shine by night like a tiny fire, and on a dull day 'you saw it as if it were in your hand'. One of the custodians of the Shrine, advancing with a silver wand, would point out the more important gems, announcing their donors — and their cost. There was certainly nothing exclusively spiritual about the Shrine of St. Thomas. And yet there was power. The evidence suggests that seldom in the history of the world has there been a greater concentration of psychic forces in one place.

Presumably the monk with the wand, unless the pilgrim in question happened to be sufficiently important to be shown round by the Prior himself, was one of the two custodians of the Shrine, appointed to watch over it by day and by night. A remarkable fifteenth century document entitled *Custumal of the Shrine of St. Thomas* has recently been acquired by the British Museum. This goes into innumerable details, hitherto generally unknown, relating to such matters as its spring-cleaning once a year, during which time the canopy was removed to the south-east transept where it stood on the site now occupied by the imposing figure of Archbishop Tait. The candles, we are told, were green, red, gold, spangled and striped. An enormous Paschal candle, presented by the town of Dover, lasted three years and had to be rolled all the way from Dover to Canterbury in a drum, since there was no other way of hauling so weighty an object.

Naturally the work of the finest glaziers, jewellers, wood carvers and metal workers had been enlisted to do honour to the saint. The Shrine itself was the work of two outstanding artists: Walter of Colchester and Elias de Dereham. The former was sacrist of St. Albans; the latter a Canon of Salisbury Cathedral. Overlooking the spot on three sides, the twelve 'Miracle' windows filled the curve of the ambulatory, more jewel-like than the jewels themselves, smouldering out of the shadows, as the nine still remaining continue to do, a source of endless delight with their frequently hilarious tales (to be worked out nowadays with the aid of binoculars, at the cost of a crick in the neck).

In its own way as beautiful and intriguing, the *Opus Alexandrinum* decorates the floor of the chapel at the head of the central flight of steps. This mosaic pavement was a gift from the Pope. The marbles are said to have been shipped to England from a storehouse at Ostia, near Rome, which housed the remains of the old pagan temples destroyed in the reign of Constantine to make way for the Church. Probably they were accompanied by the craftsmen who eventually assembled them. A fascinating analysis of the geometry of this pavement has been produced by Mr. Colin Dudley[1] in an article published in the Canterbury Cathedral Chronicle in 1969. This may serve as an introduction. The whole subject of the relationship between theology and mathematics would require volumes for its proper elucidation; moreover it is highly unlikely that anyone any longer knows a great deal about it. The *Opus Alexandrinum* is an affair of squares and circles, like any other mandala, such as for instance the Taj Mahal and the Pantheon in Rome and the sacred initiation patterns of Tibet. The circle is a symbol of perfection. It represents the heavens, over against the square which is the material universe transformed into the Kingdom of God. Anyone who wishes to play gently with such matters, not taking himself too seriously (although the subject itself is deeply serious) should read Plato and the neo-platonists — or visit the Himalayan foothills, or simply gaze at the *Opus Alexandrinum* until something of its meaning begins to unfold itself.

[1] *Sacred Geometry*. Colin Dudley. Canterbury Cathedral Chronicle. No. 64. 1969.

Opposite
The Opus Alexandrinum.

Right
'One can even stand in
front of the picture, actually
looking for it, and still not
see it.' The Knight on
horseback guarding the
entrance to the Eastern
Crypt.

The same person will probably be alerted by the extraordinary
graffiti dating from the twelfth century, which are discoverable in
various odd corners of the Cathedral, particularly in what used to
be the vicinity of the Shrine and of the tomb in the Crypt.

All Gothic Cathedrals have masons' marks, of course. Canterbury
is full of them: crosses of all kinds, letters of the alphabet, arrows,
geometrical figures: the most casual search will quickly find
examples of all these. How does one know them from the equally
numerous scratchings of petty-minded individuals with an itch to
scrawl on walls? Simply, oddly enough, because they are beautiful.

Those hair-line figures are nothing like the crude, wounding strokes made by a vandal's penknife. But the really stupendous graffiti are not masons' marks at all. They are pictures, quite large ones, many of them having something to do with St. John. Looking for them is like a game of 'hunt-the-thimble'. Sometimes it turns into that other game of trying to see faces which one knows are there, in a picture which appears to be of something else. One can pass the north wall of the passage way leading from the Western to the Eastern Crypt a thousand times without seeing the knight on horse-back; one can even stand in front of the picture, actually looking for it, and still not see it: and yet when one does see it, it is so very plain. How did it ever succeed in concealing itself? Who is this knight on this so delightful, cheerful-looking horse? Does he have something to do with the Knights of the Order of St. John?

An even more disconcerting experience awaits one on the south side, as one is about to leave this part of the Crypt. Here one is liable to be stopped in one's tracks, suddenly made aware of being face to face with a steadily gazing, haloed Christ, apparently in the act of raising the consecrated Host. Meanwhile St. John is represented as the Eagle, twice in this Eastern Crypt and again on the wall of St. Gregory's chapel in the south-east transept. In his human form he appears at least eight times as he is described in the gospel account of the Last Supper, leaning on the bosom of Christ. The best example of this pairing is in the Trinity Chapel, concealed behind one of the wall-pillars of the ambulatory on the north side: one has to squeeze in between the pillar and the wall and examine the scratching with a torch. Traces of another appear on the opposite side. On the north face of Ernulf's wall at the level of one's feet as one mounts the steps from the south-west transept to the south quire aisle, eight heads can be counted, remains of a Last Supper similar to the one which, complete with jars and plates, extends the whole way round the huge girth of one of the great piers behind the Undercroft. The Last Supper and St. John are two subjects having close associations with the Christian gnostics, those persecuted mystics of the Church who (like the Sufis of Islam) were condemned for their insistence upon the ultimate annihilation of the individual soul in a total identification with God. Nowadays we know little of these 'heretics'. But tradition has it that the apocryphal *Acts of S. John*, with its mysterious account of the Last Supper as a secret initiatory rite, was the gospel of their faith. It has been said that Canterbury Cathedral is pervaded by an aroma of gnosticism. This is an unprovable assertion: those who feel it to be true, will probably accept it as self-evident; those who do not are unlikely to be convinced.

The most remarkable of all the pictorial graffiti — known as 'Christ in Majesty with the Four Evangelists', on the west wall of the Eastern Crypt — has been protected by a sheet of glass. There is a need for similar measures to be taken with them all. People do occasionally find them; and they tend to get filled in with biro, even, occasionally, to be added to: a pastime the effects of which are more difficult to eradicate than anyone who has not tried to deal with the problem is likely to appreciate. Returning to the Trinity Chapel, a particularly delicate little drawing appears behind the wall-pier adjoining the chantry chapel of King Henry IV. This depicts what appears to be a long-handled axe, its handle tapering to a point.

One more curiosity in the Trinity Chapel is the gilded crescent moon affixed to the vault immediately above the site of the Shrine, apparently the remains of some scheme of decoration which must once have been of considerable significance. One theory associates this moon with the Saracens, and suggests a decoration consisting of horsetails and flags, trophies from the crusades. Alternatively, it may have been the base of a representation of the Virgin with 'the moon under her feet'. Traces of a fifteenth century painting of the Virgin Crowned are still to be seen on the wooden panel at the foot of the tomb of King Henry IV. Professor Tristram made a reconstruction of this painting (hanging now on the north wall of the ambulatory) which shows such a moon, identical with the one in the vault.

A number of important personages are buried in the Trinity chapel. Of these tombs, the oldest and, in its dignified simplicity, by far the most beautiful is that of Archbishop Hubert Walter, who was there before St. Thomas himself.

Hubert Walter had been Archbishop of Canterbury and Justiciar of England: a man of exceptional power and influence. In the absence of the King, when Richard I was captured and held prisoner on his way back from the Crusades, he practically ruled the country, besides being instrumental in raising the enormous sum of money which secured the King's release. He lived on into the reign of King John, who welcomed his death with the exclamation: 'Now at last I am King of England.' Before all this, as Bishop of Salisbury, he himself had been a crusader with the King's army and, in the office of peacemaker, had struck up a friendship with the Sultan which seems to have been based upon mutual understanding and respect. A truce was arranged lasting three years, three months,

three weeks and three days. Saladin sent gifts to the sick King of snow-packed fruit. 'My lord,' said the Bishop to the Ruler of the 'infidel Turks' — 'if you were converted from your unbelief, there would not be two such princes in the world as King Richard and yourself.'

A head which is believed to be that of Saladin is carved upon Archbishop Walter's tomb. He wore on his finger a ring with a gnostic device. This was discovered when, in the year 1890, the tomb was rifled by the Dean and Chapter, who took possession of its more valuable contents. When the lid of the coffin was prised open, the body of the Archbishop was disclosed, arrayed in silk embroidered vestments. The strange ring was engraved with a representation of the Egyptian serpent-god, Knuphis. With the body was a priceless treasure: a chalice and paten of such beauty that one is reminded of the vessels of the Holy Myth: surely, one thinks, the Sangraal must have appeared to Sir Bors and Sir Perceval looking exactly like that. All these things, including the vestments, were removed from the tomb, together with the archiepiscopal mitre and staff, and have become museum pieces in a glass case. One feels like apologising to the Archbishop, as one strokes the smooth surface of the marble, standing beside that immensely solid-looking chest, with its line of arcading and its four anonymous heads — one of which, whether it is a portrait of Saladin or not, is oddly suggestive of the physiognomy of an 'infidel Turk'.

This tomb stands against the wall of the ambulatory on the south side. Separated from it by a few yards is that of the Black Prince.

THE BLACK PRINCE, the nation's hero and the heir to the throne, had asked specifically in his Will to be buried in the Crypt. He may have been one of the two unnamed sons of King Edward III who, as children, were entrusted to the care and tutelage of Prior Hathbrand; if so, this would explain his lifelong devotion to the Cathedral, which seems to have been directed above all to the chapel of Our Lady Undercroft. There he was accustomed to kneel and pray. He decorated the sanctuary with the exquisitely carved screenwork which still today determines its peculiar character, its blend of norman stability with fourteenth century grace. Nearby is the Black Prince's Chantry, established to mark the occasion of his marriage with the 'Fair Maid of Kent'. This lady was his cousin within what were known as the prohibited degrees; in order to

Left, above
Sacred loot: the twelfth century chalice and paten from Archbishop Hubert Walter's tomb.

Left, below
The tomb of Archbishop Hubert Walter, with its enigmatical carved heads, in the south ambulatory of the Trinity Chapel. The second head from the left is said to be that of Saladin.

marry her, he was obliged to obtain a dispensation from the Pope. The establishment of his Chantry was part of the cost of this transaction. But his wishes were made clear. They were that his body was to lie before the altar of our Lady Undercroft. They were not carried out. Someone, his brother perhaps, for the old King was too old and the young prince too young to have any say in the matter, decreed that only the Trinity chapel, the place of the Shrine, was a fitting resting place for so great and honourable a prince. He must lie beside the martyr-saint.

The Black Prince was a complex character, whose real significance for us today, gazing admiringly as we must at that magnificent recumbent figure, the splendid canopy, the gilt, the shields, the row of 'achievements' hanging from the rail above – is not, after all, as an image of pure romance. This was the notion of him that was presented to several generations of schoolchildren in the heyday of British imperialism and the public school. A great soldier, a paragon of courage, chivalry and honour, a knight in shining armour: so the Victorians, Edwardians and Georgians conceived of him. Precisely how he appeared to his contemporaries is another matter. They idolised him; but rather more realistically, one suspects. Our picture of him is different again. The popular view of him has changed, as the popular view of England's past has changed. For that is the secret of the Black Prince. He is England to the English.

There are times when one mounts the steps to stand beside that tomb and what is, for the most part, a mere cerebral recognition of fact becomes for the moment a burning awareness: here, within the stretch of my arm, are the dust and bones of the man who, as a boy of sixteen, commanded the whole English army against what appeared to be impossible odds. 'Crecy' is not just a name in a history book. Crecy was a *place*. And the story comes to life.

The French King (and one can hardly wonder at it) had had enough. He had hoisted the Oriflamme: the very name of the thing conveys its splendour and its fearfulness. It was a great scarlet banner embroidered with gold lilies; and its purpose was to proclaim that the battle to be fought was to be regarded as a 'holy war' – which meant, by a dreadful irony, that no quarter would be shown, no prisoners would be taken, every man who could be so dealt with would be hewn down and slaughtered on the field – including, if possible, the King himself. King Edward, however, had seated himself prudently on the summit of a nearby hill. 'Let the boy win his spurs,' he is said to have remarked, as his young son went hallooing

'England to the English':
the Black Prince.

into the battle, to what must have seemed like almost certain death. And then came a sudden storm of rain. The bows of the French archers were soaked and useless. In later years the Prince's badge was a sun emerging from behind a cloud, as it did that day, metaphorically as well as literally, for him at least. On the day following the victory the King and his son strolled together through the field of carnage. 'What think you of a battle?' inquired the King. 'Is it an agreeable game?'

Apparently the Prince did think so. At the age of twenty-six he captured the French King at Poitiers, after which he dined and wined the poor man, serving him with his own hands and on bended knee. 'Sir,' said the Black Prince (so called because his servants' livery was black, or because the plumes in his helm were black, or because the French called him *Le Prince Noir*, the Prince of Darkness: Cathedral guides may take their choice) – 'for God's sake make no bad cheer, though your will was not accomplished this day. For Sir, the King my father will certainly bestow on you as much honour and friendship as he can, and will agree with you so reasonably that you shall ever after be friends; and Sir, I think you ought to rejoice though the battle be not as you will, for you have this day gained the high honour of prowess and have surpassed all others on your side in valour. Sir, I say not this in trickery, for all our party who saw every man's deeds agree in this and give to you the palm and chaplet.'

It is a little difficult to see how the French King could be expected to smile pleasantly at this self-possessed young man, who bore the French arms quarterly on his own shield, and whose father calmly designated himself the King of England and France (passing down this title to his successors until the reign of George III). In any case he was obliged to return to England with the Prince, who took his prisoner straight to Canterbury, himself riding a small black pony as they came into the city, with the King on a magnificent charger towering above him, physically if not in any other respect. The two royal visitors made offerings at the Shrine and were given appropriate entertainment. One more King was humiliated in Canterbury while the people gaped.

The Prince lived to the age of forty-six. He was a grievously sick man for some years before his death. Unable to support himself upon his feet, the hero of Crecy and Poitiers was carried in a litter through the streets of Limoges, the 'rebel' town whose fearful punishment had been directly ordered by himself. Every man, woman and child was being butchered systematically from street to street. The dying and those who knew they must shortly die, recognised him and held out their arms to him as the litter passed. 'Mercy!' they cried. 'Mercy!' But he had no mercy. He too was a dying man. He was staring, one imagines, at his own death. Four years later, on Trinity Sunday in the year 1376, his household at Westminster gathered round him, and he commended to them his little son, the child who in a very short time (for Edward III was dying too) would be the new King. As Eliot transposed the final words of Becket into verse, so did the poet and herald Sir John Chandos, those of the Black Prince:

I recommend to you my son
Who is yet but young and small
And pray that as you served me
So from your heart you would serve him.

The poet, who was himself an eye-witness of the scene, succeeds

Opposite
An old man strays among the tombs. This nineteenth century print depicts the Trinity Chapel in a moment of silence and peace. Note the tomb of Archbishop Hubert Walter on the left and that of Odet de Coligny on the right.

in convincing us that this is no merely conventional, sycophantic account:

But till then so God aid me
Never was seen so bitter grief
As was at his departure
For he prayed God for mercy
And pardon for all his misdeeds
That he had done in this world
And then the Prince passed away
From this world and so died
At the noble City of London
On the high day of Trinity
Which through all his life
He had kept holy with melody.

The funeral was three months later on Michaelmas Day. Archbishop Simon of Sudbury welcomed the procession and celebrated the Requiem Mass. The tomb had already been made: the marble table, the enamelled shields, the impressive figure, every detail of which had been described in the Prince's Will: 'an image of latten . . . all armed in steel for battle with our arms quartered; and my visage with our helmet of the leopard put under the head of the image'. The Prince had not mentioned the cheerful little dog which supports the feet. Above the tomb on an iron railing hung what were known as his 'achievements'. These were his jupon, shield, sword, gauntlets, helm and cap of maintenance with the lion (sometimes called the leopard) crest. The sword has since disappeared. Shortly after the Second World War, the remaining objects were put in a glass case for preservation, and copies of them were made to be hung in their place. These copies are exceedingly handsome and accurate. The jupon of silk nylon-velvet has the arms of England and France embroidered in gold thread. It was made by the Royal School of Needlework, their next major undertaking after the Coronation robe of our present Queen. The 'achievements' are generally regarded as being of sensational interest. Like all other durable objects which were made at that time, they are examples of the finest craftsmanship; however, they are insignificant in comparison with the smudged remains of a painting on the underside of the wooden canopy above the recumbent figure of the Prince. On account of its position this picture can never have been easy to look at, being intended solely as an object of devotion for the Prince himself. Professor Tristram working extensively in the Cathedral in the nineteen-thirties, made a reconstruction of this painting which hangs now on the south wall of the ambulatory, a few yards from

'... an odd resemblance ... to his descendant, King Edward VII.' King Henry IV and his Queen, Joan of Navarre.

the tomb. Beautiful and strange, it depicts the Eternal Father seated upon a rainbow, holding the Crucified Son against His breast. At the four corners are the symbols of the Four Evangelists. Tristram has added the figure of the Third Person of the Trinity in the form of a Dove. This does appear in a number of contemporary paintings of this type. On the other hand, there is a small fourteenth century badge in the British Museum, depicting the Black Prince in prayer before an almost identical figure of the Father and the Son, without the Dove. This group is surrounded by a garter inscribed with the words (which also appear upon the tomb) *hony soyt ke mal y pense*.

The most important individual in the group surrounding the Prince's deathbed was his younger brother, the Duke of Lancaster, Shakespeare's 'old John of Gaunt'. It is said that he 'swore upon the book' to comfort the young Richard, heir to the throne, and 'maintain him in his right'. Perhaps it was not his fault that it was his own son, Henry, who took from this same Richard the Crown of England and was almost certainly responsible for his death. Now they lie together, separated only by the space which once contained the Shrine: Richard's father, the Black Prince, and King Henry IV.

Henry IV is the only monarch to be buried in Canterbury Cathedral, which has generally been held to represent the Ecclesiastical authority as distinct from that of the State. Why he made a point of choosing this place of internment for himself, we do not know. In addition to the ordering of his tomb, he left instructions in his Will for the erection of a chantry chapel to be built out from the north wall, a few yards away from the tomb itself. This chapel would be served, as was customary, by two priests who would celebrate masses in perpetuity for the King's soul and for that of Queen Joan. The tomb was not finished until shortly before the Queen's death in 1437, twenty-four years after that of the King. It is constructed of alabaster with a wooden canopy: the figures of the King and Queen lie side by side, the jewels of their coronets and the fine embroidery of their royal robes delicately and accurately portrayed, while the faces are obviously portraits, that of King Henry bearing an odd resemblance, frequently remarked upon (and invariably found useful as a subject of polite conversation on royal visits), to his descendant, King Edward VII.

In 1832 the tomb was opened by order of the Dean and Chapter, for the purpose of refuting a rather silly rumour that the King's body had been thrown overboard by sailors on its way to Faversham. Two leaden coffins were found beneath the monument. That of the King being prised open, a quantity of haybands was revealed and, lying upon these, a tiny cross formed of two twigs tied together — which, most regrettably, fell to pieces on being moved. Beneath the haybands was another coffin. An oval piece of this was removed and, in the words of one of the Canons who was an eye-witness of the scene: 'to the astonishment of all present the face of the deceased King was seen in complete preservation, the nose elevated, the cartilege even remaining; though on the admission of the air it sunk rapidly away, and had entirely disappeared before the examination was finished. The skin of the chin was entire . . . the beard thick and matted and of a deep russet colour'.

The family party in the Trinity Chapel consisted, by the year 1437, of the King and Queen; the King's uncle, the Black Prince; his half-brother, the Earl of Somerset; and his second son, the Duke of Clarence: the two latter being the successive husbands of a certain Margaret Holland, an enterprising lady who was planning for herself a *mènage à trois* in the south-west transept. The Earl of Somerset was a Beaufort. He was the son of John of Gaunt and his mistress Kathryn Swynford, whose children, the Beauforts, were legitimised when the old Duke eventually made Kathryn his third wife. Margaret's idea was to construct a magnificent tomb bearing the

Opposite
'. . . polyandrous peace':
Lady Margaret Holland and
her two husbands, the
Earl of Somerset and the
Duke of Clarence.

BENEATH THIS STONE ARE
DEPOSITED THE BODY OF
CHARLOTTE WIFE OF

recumbent effigies of her two husbands and herself. To this end she ordered the removal of the tomb of Archbishop Stephen Langton, which had to be pushed through the east wall of the chapel, half in and half out. The great Archbishop who was principally respons-ible for the signing of Magna Carta, was obliged to give place to a strong-minded lady with a fat purse. The result is a splendidly ostentatious monument. The three figures are admirable examples of the realistic rendering in alabaster of flowing draperies, jewellery, armour, and the softness of human flesh. On the 18th December 1439 the work was completed: eleven days later the twice-widowed lady died: the bodies of Somerset and Clarence were exhumed under the auspices of the Prior, and the three were united in what appears to be polyandrous peace.

In the Trinity Chapel one more tomb deserves to be pointed out. A bare mound of brickwork roughly plastered over with cement, it houses the coffin of Odet de Coligny, Bishop of Beauvais and Cardinal de Châtillon. The Cardinal, along with many others, had fled to England in the year 1568 to escape the Huguenot persecu-tions in France. High dignitary of the Church as he was, he was suspected of being at heart a Protestant. Three years later he was in Canterbury contemplating the possibility of returning to his own country, when he died suddenly and mysteriously — some said of poison administered in an apple by one of his servants. No one seems to have bothered at all about his tomb. It was vaguely sup-posed that his body would be 'sent for' but it never was. In recent years a plaque has been erected to indicate the identity of the occupant of this strange sarcophagus. An 'audio-guide' (now mercifully removed) in the form of a telephone, which stood beside it for some years, reminded one absurdly that the poor man had been awaiting for centuries a call which never came. He continues to wait; and now the very oddness of his tomb has become interesting and will be left exactly as it is.

THE STORY of Odet de Coligny belongs to the reign of Queen Elizabeth. By that time, all traces of the Shrine of St. Thomas had been razed from the pavement of the Trinity Chapel by order of King Henry VIII. The Regale had disappeared from history, having spent some time on the King's thumb-ring, reappeared briefly on a collar worn by his daughter Mary, and then vanished, with the bones of St. Thomas, without trace. Were those bones thrown (as some say) into the Stour — or reburied somewhere in the Cathedral — or

THOMAS BECKET
ARCHBISHOP · SAINT · MARTYR
DIED HERE
TUESDAY 29TH·DECEMBER
1170

This painting of the murder of Archbishop Becket, now hanging in the Martyrdom transept, is a reconstruction by Professor Tristram of the fifteenth century painting on wood at the head of the tomb of King Henry IV.

Overleaf
SW view of the Cathedral.

actually burnt? Archdeacon Nicholas Harpsfield, writing in the reign of Queen Mary, at least had no doubt: 'Albeit we have of late (God illuminate our beetle blind hearts to see and repent our folly and impiety!) unshrined him and burned his holy bones. . . .'

Besides the Regale, the following items were among those which had been plundered from the Cathedral by the King: five thousand ounces of gold, four thousand of gilt plate, five thousand of silver-gilt, five thousand of plain silver, twenty-six cartloads of jewels, four precious mitres, nine pontifical rings, eleven copes of gold cloth called 'gold Bawdekin', one covering for an altar 'of white and red velvet splendidly worked'. The present Dean and Chapter, appealing desperately for three million pounds to preserve the Cathedral in existence, could make good use of all that; furiously as they would be criticised for doing so, no doubt. One marvels that anything was left; and yet we are not led to suppose that the Cathedral was grievously impoverished: on the contrary it would appear that the King, having sated his cupidity and got rid of the monks, dealt fairly by it according to his own peculiar lights.

The cult of St. Thomas had been fading before that, if not positively falling into disrepute. Erasmus, after visiting the Cathedral barely twenty-five years before the destruction of the Shrine, described his experience in terms of quiet civilised humour, which speak to us now of the new age which was dawning, for better or for worse. The distinguished humanist and his companion Dean Colet, having been conducted from one to another of the altars of St. Thomas, were far from delighted by the 'parcel of ragged handkerchiefs with marks upon them of having been used' which the Prior was expecting them to kiss. Colet went so far as to accept one of these unattractive objects between his finger and thumb and then lay it down hastily with a whistle of disgust. Prior Goldston II tactfully pretended not to notice. Erasmus blushed.

Shortly after this episode the Priory were in trouble in connection with the Holy Maid (not to be confused with the Fair one) of Kent. This poor girl, a maid servant in the employment of a family living near Aldington, had the misfortune to be a natural psychic. In the sixteenth century one went into mediumistic trances at one's peril. If, in the course of those trances, one was so extremely unfortunate as to utter ringing criticisms of the monarch, relating to the touchy subject of his private life, one might as well have been dead from the start. To make matters worse, there were always those who took advantage of such phenomena, even at considerable personal risk. The poor Maid, whose name was Elizabeth Barton, was brought to

Canterbury, to the nunnery of St. Sepulchre, where various persons sought to exploit her 'powers' in a vain attempt to stop the King's divorce. There is even a story that she was brought secretly to the Cathedral and there immured in a kind of hole above the Deans' Chapel, whence her voice was made to issue through a small opening, uttering maledictions against the King and his mistress in the strange tones associated with the state of trance. There is no substantial evidence for this tale. But Dr. Bocking, the warden of the Christ Church manors, and Richard Dering, the cellarer, were her constant associates. All three ended their lives on the scaffold; and Prior Goldwell was hard put to it to appease the royal wrath.

Poor Prior Goldwell: when the blow at last fell and Christ Church Priory, in common of course with all the other Religious foundations in the country at that time, was dissolved by order of the King, he addressed a letter to Cromwell in a last pathetic bid to remain in his own Cathedral and his own house. Rumours have reached him, he says, that a certain Dr. Thorneden was being spoken of as the new Dean, which office 'by favour of your good lordship I trusted to have had, and as yet trust to have. I have been prior of the said church above 22 years. It hath also been shown unto me that my lord of Canterbury at his coming to the said church will take from me the keys of my chamber, and if he do I doubt whether I shall have the same keys or chamber again or not. . . . And whereas it pleased your good mind towards me to write unto me of late, by your letters, that I should have my said chamber with all commodities of the same as I have had in times past, the which your said writing to me was, and is, much to my comfort. And with the favour of your lordship I trust so to have for the term of my life, which term of my life by course of nature cannot be long, for I am above the age of 62 years.' [1]

In the event neither Goldwell nor Thorneden became the first Dean of the new foundation. Goldwell was provided with an adequate pension and lived to the age of seventy-seven, a very old man by the standards of those times. The first Dean of Canterbury was Nicholas Wotton, whose ornate monument adjoins that of King Henry IV. Dean Wotton would appear to have been an able diplomat rather than a conscientious cleric. He was employed on a number of successful embassies in the service of the State; and he must have used his diplomatic abilities to some purpose on his own account. Through four reigns, while heads rolled and martyrs burned, Catholic and Protestant in turn being faced with the choice between recantation and a horrible death, the Dean of Canterbury and York

[1] Quoted in W. & D.

retained his two commodious and lucrative appointments. Pluralism and absenteeism were taken to be a matter of course. The 'Church of England', compromising, solid, having its own peculiar dignity, flexibility, imperviousness and charm, was in the process of becoming established. A Dean and twelve Canons ruled at Canterbury. (Nowadays there are four Canons, but the general set-up has not radically changed.)

No sooner were they all appointed than they started squabbling (one is tempted to say that they have gone on ever since). They squabbled over their own particular NEB. The New English Bible as it was then, forerunner of the Authorised Version of 1611, had been introduced into the Cathedral by order of King Henry VIII. A copy of it was chained to a desk in the north quire aisle. There is still a chained Bible on this desk. Its date is 1572. By that time things had begun to settle down. The Bible in English was no longer so great a cause of offence as it had been once.

We are not told if they squabbled over the coal cellar in the Crypt. For centuries William the Englishman's superb chapel was used by the dignitaries of the Cathedral as a fuel dump. They built themselves houses out of, and in some cases around and above, the ruined walls of the monastic buildings; with the result that some of those walls, which would otherwise almost certainly have vanished sooner or later, emerged when the houses which incorporated them were eventually pulled down. At this point — apart from a few excitements, such as were provided by the Puritan soldiery and Blue Dick with his ladder and his pike — a mist seems to come down and linger for a very long time. It is not that we do not know what happened; but that what happened seems less extraordinary, less important. The riotous colours are subdued. The shrill medieval instruments are gone. The *Opus Dei* becomes Mattins and Evensong and 'Holy Communion'. The monastery becomes the Precincts. As the centuries pass, we begin to hear the swishing skirts of Canons' wives, as the rooks caw and the pigeons coo on Christ Church Gate. Neat little houses, cooing pigeons, cawing rooks, the ceremonious lifting of cockaded hats. . . .

But the Cathedral does not change. It holds its being within itself.

THE OLDEST part of the Cathedral now is Ernulf's Crypt. This Western Crypt, divided from that of William the Englishman by an apsidal arrangement of tremendously solid-looking piers before which stands the altar of Our Lady Undercroft, is dim and spacious and cool. Entering it, one is instantly possessed by a feeling of peace. It has never (until now) been used, like William's Crypt, for any secular purpose. For centuries after the dissolution, it was the place of worship of the French Huguenot refugees, until their numbers diminished and they retired into the Chantry chapel of their country's old enemy, the Black Prince. In the Second World War the Crypt was converted into an air-raid shelter; and no place could have been better calculated to calm the fears of those who made use of it. Temporarily, at the time of writing (1976) it is partially taken up by an Exhibition in aid of the Cathedral Appeal. A small part of it will eventually be used as a treasury, housing a valuable collection of altar furnishings, Communion vessels and embroidered vestments, including of course the exquisite objects from the Hubert Walter tomb. So it will return to itself; and there is reason to suppose that its essential character will be respected and, at least in the foresee-able future, it will be left as it is. One would like to see it used (if there is any real need for it to be 'used' at all) as a setting for Religious Drama and Dance, perhaps also for 'ecumenical' worship in the widest possible sense, which would include the sacred ceremonies of other great religions: a vital innovation at this time when we are beginning at last to understand the principle of unity underlying all the valid rites.

The somewhat gnomic character of Ernulf's Crypt is created by its fantastic carvings, executed in 1096 in the Cathedral workshop. Of the piers upholding the nave, alternate shafts and capitals are richly and curiously adorned. The four faces of each carved capital present a motley collection of mythical creatures engaged in strange dances, the origin and significance of which are lost in the depths of the past. One gets used to being told that the masons were just 'having fun' in the Crypt; but although they were undoubtedly having fun, it is highly improbable that they did not understand the import of their fun. Now we can do little more than gaze in wonder-ment. A gnomic being with long ears, the lower part of his torso turned back to front, straddles the backsides of a pair of horse-like creatures with immensely long tails; he grasps them by their noses while they swivel their heads round in protest. A delightful lion smiles benignly as if in affectionate amusement. Two unidentifiable creatures (donkeys? – rabbits? – dogs? – but they both have long tails and one is winged) play musical instruments. Most extra-ordinary of all is a lion with four wings, a pair of human arms and

Opposite, right
Capitals in St. Gabriel's Chapel.

Opposite, left
Twelfth century capitals in Ernulf's Crypt.

Druidic know-how or just having fun? Musical animals in St. Gabriel's Chapel.

two human heads. One of the heads has curved horns like a ram's and what appears to be a drooping moustache: the face has the look of a kindly old gentleman in a club, who has just woken up. The right hand holds a fish, while the left bears a shallow dish containing what appears to be either pellets of bread or small fruits. A girdle of flames suggests some connection, if not identification, with the sun.

Elsewhere in the Crypt, St. Gabriel's chapel has a particularly fine example of a capital representing 'musical animals', in this case a snouted creature with horns and cloven hooves, standing upright and playing a fiddle, while a seated donkey tootles happily on a trumpet. Of 'musical animals' in general, as they appear in Gothic Cathedrals, the nearest approach to an explanation seems to be contained in *The Mysteries of Chartres Cathedral* by Louis Charpentier, who writes:

There are on the southern wall of the South tower two highly damaged carvings: an ass holding an instrument of music and another animal, standing on its hind legs, whose head and front parts have disappeared. According to oral tradition, this is 'the Ass that plays the hurdy-gurdy' and the 'Sow that spins'. The Sow is visibly a boar and the hurdy-gurdy a kind of cithern.

'What a strange thing', Canon Bulteau writes, 'there is to be seen on a document from ancient Egypt, an ass that plucks (the French word is "pince" and the author himself queries it) a lyre with nine strings.' Egypt again.

The ass is perhaps an onager, an animal which in antiquity had some symbolical meaning I have been unable to find. There are at least two 'asses' that are stars in the constellation of Cancer and for the Egyptians the ass symbolised Typhon, a god of evil.

Were we concerned with no more than a small carved stone we might have allowed ourselves to assume some malicious trick on the part of some sculptor who meant to mock those who are always wishful to do for music what they are as little fitted to do as the donkey, the harmony of whose voice is well known. But this piece of sculpture is of too much consequence for there to be any question of a joke. And then, there is the sow or boar, as to which we are better informed. The word *truie* is a variation of an ancient Celtic word (truth) that means *wild boar*. Truth, by phonetic assimilation, was one of the images of the Druid, not the only one: another was the oak, *dru*; yet another was connected with the trout. The 'boar that spins' is the Druid who draws a guiding thread from the distaff, like Ariadne's. Was there a tradition among the building confraternities of a druidic know-how carefully preserved in the tricks of their trade and its jargon? Certain survivals of Gaulish art, above all in romanesque architecture, make one think so.[1]

Is the standing creature in St. Gabriel's chapel a kind of boar? It could be so. We must leave it at that.

[1] *The Mysteries of Chartres Cathedral* by Louis Charpentier. Trans. Ronald Fraser in collaboration with Janette Jackson. Research into Lost Knowledge Organisation. 1972.

[2] There seems to be some difference of opinion on the extent to which the Quire and Trinity Chapel were adorned with painting at the time or shortly after they were built. One art historian assured me: 'Hardly at all'; on the other hand Professor Tristram (Address to the Friends of Canterbury Cathedral, June 1935) seems to have visualised an overall treatment of the entire Cathedral at that date. Traces remain here and there. It is not for me to enter into a discussion of the subject. One thing, however, is certain: Gothic builders, in contrast to those of the Romanesque period, were far more concerned with geometry than with pictorial decoration.

THE ORIGINAL heavy iron rings for the hanging lamps are still suspended from the vault of Ernulf's Crypt. Traces remain of the painted Crowns of Thorns which surrounded those rings. One has to imagine the whole of the Crypt as being gaudy and glowing with paint. We may prefer it as it is: but it was not always as it is. It was the greater sophistication characteristic of the late twelfth century and arriving in Canterbury with William of Sens, which introduced the idea that beauty could reside in the plain unpainted majesty of dressed and chiselled stone, without any overall adornment.[2] And even after that, in the thirteenth, fourteenth and fifteenth centuries, for so long as the elaborate ritual and ceremony of the Catholic Church held sway in Canterbury, a thousand objects must have contributed to the variegated colours of the scene: painted images, embroidered hangings and vestments, glittering gems on the numerous altars and shrines, the burning glory of the coloured glass, all to be seen in the tremulous glow of frequently moving candles and lamps. Lighting is not only a practical necessity but, potentially at least, the greatest of all images of Truth; although nowadays, in Canterbury Cathedral, it is of such a nature that one

Left
Shrine of the Virgin,
haven for shelterers in
World War II; the Chapel
of Our Lady Undercroft.

Opposite
One of the great supportive
piers bearing up the Quire
behind the Chapel of Our
Lady Undercroft.

would prefer to grope in the dark. Erasmus tells us of the difference which lighted tapers made to the chapel of Our Lady Undercroft. 'Here the Virgin hath an habitation,' he writes, referring to his visit to Ernulf's Crypt, 'but somewhat dark . . . light being brought, we saw a more than royal spectacle; in beauty it far surpassed that of Walsingham.'

This was the chapel beloved of the Black Prince. He it was who had given the intricately carved stone reredos and lateral screens. These, when Erasmus saw them, were painted in brilliant colours overlaid with patterns in gilt. The vault of the sanctuary was a deep blue with a powdering of gilded suns and stars slightly raised from the surface. The remains of all this splendour are visible – and beautiful – still, the colours softened, the lines a little blurred. In the tall central niche behind the altar is a seventeenth century statuette of Our Lady from Portugal, presented to the Cathedral shortly after the Second World War. The figure is far removed in style and period

from both the screenwork and the Crypt itself; but, as Crypt and screens go happily together, so does this graceful object go with them: beauty with beauty; here as elsewhere in the Cathedral, where only mediocrity and insipidity strike a jarring note.

During the war, when Ernulf's Crypt was being used as a shelter, the lives of some of the inhabitants of the Precincts were almost certainly saved as a result. It seems unbelievable now that Dean Hewlett Johnson, carrying his Chapter along with him for once, set in motion this admirable project and brought it to completion against furious opposition – chiefly, let it be added, from those who either did not live nearby or were about to move hastily somewhere else. In his autobiography *Searching for Light*, the Dean has described this episode, quoting from an open letter which was sent to all members of the 'Friends of Canterbury Cathedral'. The following extract from this letter tells the story of what took place:

In the war of 1914–18, the Crypt was the shelter in which young and old found refuge. Justifiably the Dean and Chapter concluded that it would be so used again, but that clearly it was not strong enough to withstand modern explosive weapons. Under expert advice, including that of Sir Charles Peers, they sandbagged the sides of the Crypt, shored up the ceiling and provided amenities. But we were informed by those qualified to speak, that the Crypt ceiling was too thin to withstand masonry that might crash upon it. Therefore, under the guidance of expert advisers, the Dean and Chapter caused steel girders to be placed over the aisles out-side the Choir which should bear some feet of earth to act as a cushion to prevent masonry crashing through on to people taking refuge below. No one knew how much or how little time was available, and the quickest method was clearly the best; the earth was dry and might not long remain so. Hence an automatic digger was hired, rails put down in the Nave and trolleys run into the Choir with dry earth to be distributed into the aisles at the sides.

Opposite
This seventeenth century ivory statuette from Portugal, representing Our Lady in Glory, has recently been placed in the central niche of the reredos above the altar of Our Lady Undercroft.

During this work the Nave and Choir presented a sad spectacle, and unhappily people photographed the site and published the pictures with-out authority; bitter letters were written to the press and 'desecration' was the common word. It is the wrong word, however, for public worship has gone on daily, the musical services have been fully maintained, additional services are held, and meetings for intercession are frequent in the week. Within a very short time from now the Nave and the Choir will have been cleaned and will present their normal aspect; the Chapels will be open, clean, furnished and in use. The only 'desecration' will be in the fact that two short corridors outside the Choir now form a cushion of earth.[1]

[1] *Searching for Light*. Hewlett Johnson. Michael Joseph. 1968.

The campaign against this essential work reached such a pitch that the Nazi Government came to know of it, and German leaders spoke publicly of Canterbury Cathedral as having been 'fortified' against attack.

The smoking city as seen
from the top of Bell Harry
Tower on the morning
following the June raid.

Inset
A scene of desolation near
the Cathedral.

At the same time, and to the accompaniment of a similar chorus of indignation, every pane of Canterbury's medieval glass was removed and stored away safely, most of it in St. Gabriel's Chapel in the Crypt. After the war, it was put back: the operation took six years and the combined knowledge and skill of the glaziers of the Cathedral workshop, notably Mr. George Easton: now it has all to be done again, since the discovery was made that Canterbury's glass is disintegrating as a result of pollution and requires expert treatment. However, had it not been for the foresight and rapid initiative of the Dean, there would have been no glass left now for us to worry about.

Important tombs were buried beneath mounds of sandbagging at this time. It is odd to remember how entirely the Cathedral retained its character, with its windows gone, its important monuments covered up, and great banks of boarded up sandbagging protecting the Crypt. A single obtrusive 'audio-bar' or 'mike' can damage its atmosphere more really than all these necessary precautions ever did; indeed they damaged nothing: the Presence of the Cathedral was never more intensely present.

T HERE W AS never a great crowd of shelterers in the Crypt. When it became apparent, early on, that the Cathedral itself was a target, people living outside the Precincts naturally avoided it during alerts. On the other hand, those who lived close by continued to use it, at intervals, especially at night. There was comfort in those solid piers and walls; comfort, too, of another kind, which no one who has not run in terror through the south door and down the half-lit steps to the waiting shrine of Our Lady Undercroft, will be able fully to understand. In 1940, however, the worst of the raids were still to come; and a small number of regular shelterers came every night through the blackout and the ever open Gate. These were incorporated into the cast of Martin Browne's *Mime of Christmas*, performed that year in Ernulf's Crypt. The principal movers of this event were Father Geoffrey Keable and his wife from St. George's church.

The ancient church of St. George the Martyr was burned to the ground in the June raid of 1942. It had, naturally, many links with the Cathedral, one of which was the friendship which existed in the· thirties and during the war between its Rector and Canterbury's Dean. Both men, on account of their socialist views, were targets of

intemperate fury on the part of a certain section of the city's inhabitants. During the war, however, this section was noticeably diminished. The Dean and Father Keable, together with Joseph Poole who was in charge of the music, were jointly responsible for an event which no one who had anything to do with it is ever likely to forget.

A number of highly professional dramatic performances have taken place in the Chapter House, and some in the Cathedral itself. This was not a professional performace. The cast, apart from those regular shelterers, was drawn from the group of young people who, at that time, were the leaven of St. George's church. Traditional carols were sung. The Nativity story was read from the Authorised Version of the New Testament. There was no 'acting', only a relaxed and carefully formalised miming of the Sacred Myth. The costumes, lent by the 'Friends', belonged to the period of Memlinc and Van Eyck; so that Mary appeared, in her heavy russet-coloured dress with enormous hanging sleeves, exactly as she does in a typical Flemish altarpiece. The words, the music, the beauty of the setting, the loving involvement of those taking part — at a time when, in any case, only the essential things were regarded as being important — made of that Christmas Eve a kind of trysting place where time and eternity seemed to meet. The extent of the actors' involvement had its comical aspects. One delightful old man, a Canterbury 'character' who kept an antique shop in the Butter market and was always known as 'Boy Blue' on account of his sky blue plus fours, was given the part of a King. Such was his identification with this character that he took to bowing profoundly, with the air of one in possession of an esoteric secret, whenever he encountered 'Mary' in the street. 'Mary', being very young, was a trifle abashed.

Before the war ended, very different scenes were to be enacted in the same place. 'Mary' had another part to play, when she left the Crypt at four-thirty one summer's morning, to make tea in her own house in the Precincts, and come back with it on a tray, for her mother, three old ladies and a dog. A night of fear had been followed by a dawn of relief, as the All Clear sounded and, beyond the boarded-up windows of the Crypt, birds in the Precincts began to chirp. The wires of the barrage balloons hummed, as they sank to the ground, on a high continuous note. They were latecomers, those balloons. Four of them guarded the Cathedral; but only after the June raid had drawn attention to its perilously unguarded state. One of them had its base in the Green Court where it lay like a grounded fish between the periods of alert. To 'Mary', the experience of hurrying across the

Precincts with a tray of teathings in the soft cool air of the dawn, and then of dispensing tea in the Crypt to four ladies and a small dog, seemed natural enough. Nothing in those days was 'odd': not even a dog drinking tea out of a thin china saucer at a quarter to five in the morning in the Chapel of our Lady Undercroft.

THERE ARE six chapels in Ernulf's Crypt. These are the Undercroft, St. Gabriel's, the Holy Innocents, the two apsidal chapels of the north transept, and the Chantry of the Black Prince.

The Black Prince's Chantry was originally two chapels, constituting the south transept. Basically it is a norman structure entirely covered by a skin of perpendicular stonework. There are some pleasing fourteenth century bosses, one representing Samson and the

Joan Wake, Fair Maid of Kent, portrayed in the Chantry Chapel of her husband, the Black Prince.

Lion, another the Pelican tearing her breast to feed her young. A third is the head of a rather plain, square-faced lady who is supposed to be the Fair Maid herself: Joan Holland, Joan Plantagenet – Joan Wake. Joan, who was Baroness Wake in her own right, had inherited her title from her uncle, her mother's brother, who belonged to the ancient family of Wake which claims its descent from Hereward through the female line.[1] Her soubriquet of 'the Fair

[1] Joan's connection with the Wake family may be checked from the account of this family in Burkes Peerage.

Maid' is misleading. The Black Prince was her third husband. Not only was he his cousin; but – and surely this was an even more pressing reason for that dispensation from the Pope – at the time of their marriage she had a divorced husband still living. (The parallels between Edward the Black Prince and Edward Duke of Windsor, who likewise died on Trinity Sunday, are so numerous as to be worth the consideration of anyone who is intrigued by 'co-incidence'.)

The Black Prince's Chantry Chapel is still, today, the French Huguenot church. The first Protestant refugees from the continent arrived in Canterbury at the beginning of the sixteenth century. For the next two hundred years (excepting the short interval of Mary's reign) waves of immigrants took refuge in Protestant England from the savagery of the persecutions in France. In Paris, Protestant ministers were being tortured on the wheel in public squares. In Canterbury there was a haven of peace. Some time during the year 1547, one Strypes (described as 'an analyst') committed to paper the following happy observation, which deserves to be quoted annually, having never ceased to be appropriate:

'I find divers outlandish and godly men this year at Canterbury.'

The divers outlandish and godly men, on this occasion, were Walloons and Huguenots. It seems to have been Archbishop Cranmer who took the initiative in extending a positive welcome to these immigrants. For obvious reasons, however, it was not until the reign of Elizabeth that the French Protestant community became firmly established, and large numbers of refugees began to be attracted by the prospect of a secure future for themselves and their descendants. Many went to London, of course; but many stopped by on their way. There was a welcome in Canterbury – and a place of worship. They must have been very tired, and very thankful to stop when they could. It is said that one large band of them, arriving at Sandwich and proceeding to Canterbury, when they came in sight of Bell Harry in the distance, began to sing psalms, and so entered the city as Augustine and his monks had done, singing the praises of God.

There is no record of the date on which this Protestant community came firmly into possession of the Crypt. The privilege was confirmed to them by Order in Council in 1662, but this was no more than the legal ratification of a situation already in existence. For a long time they occupied Ernulf's Crypt in its entirety (William's, it will be remembered, was by this time a wood cellar and general storage dump). In the city they set up a prosperous weaving industry, and for a time the community multiplied; but then, inevitably, it merged with the local population and the congregation diminished. Around the year 1895 it retreated into the Black Prince's Chantry, which is known today as the Huguenot church. It presents a curious mixture of influences, with its norman basis, perpendicular overlay and evangelical furnishings. Services continue to be held there every Sunday in French.

In the city itself innumerable family names derive from those immigrants. Baker may originally have been Boulanger; Terry, Thierry; Wood, Dubois: and so forth. But the best known Huguenot name in Canterbury is Lefevre. Frederick Charles Lefevre was Mayor of Canterbury all through the Second World War and died in office. The name 'Huguenot' itself is said to have been applied to the French Protestants because they met in the city of Tours by a certain gate known as Huguet. This gate was called after King Huguet, villain of a medieval romance. The city of Tours was reputed to be haunted by his ghost.

THE TWO chapels corresponding to the Black Prince's Chantry on the north side are those of St. Mary Magdalene and St. Nicholas. Both have been recently restored. They are open chapels, consisting in each case of an apsidal sanctuary, the chord of which is spanned by a norman arch. Both have windows of thirteenth century glass from a private collection purchased by the Dean and Chapter shortly after the Second World War for the purpose of filling in empty windows in the south quire aisle and in the Crypt. The Chapel of St. Nicholas was restored by Julian and Burgon Bickersteth in memory of their parents. Julian Bickersteth was Archdeacon of Maidstone and Canon Residentiary of the Cathedral from 1943 until his death in 1962. To recall his ministry is an act of justice. In view of the constant criticisms levelled against the Cathedral clergy for being 'uncaring' and 'remote', it is only fair to redress the balance.

The Cathedral does not provide its clergy with a parish. They have to find their own means of service; and not infrequently, in the past, they have given the impression of withdrawing into the elitist world of the Precincts, a world which tends to look odder from the outside than those within can easily appreciate. There used to be two Archdeacons on the governing body of the Cathedral. Nowadays there is one. They, at least, have always had plenty to do. But they too can seem to be inaccessible from the point of view of the ordinary citizen, if only on account of the load of administrative duties which constitutes their work. Archdeacon Bickersteth was not a young man when he came to Canterbury. Arriving with a long career behind him in the field of education, he assumed not only the duties of his archdeaconry but those of Chairman of the Diocesan Education Committee and various other responsible positions in the area of his particular interest. He gave of himself to the Cathedral in innumerable ways. He it was, for instance, who devised and put into operation the scheme whereby clergy of the diocese were commissioned as honorary chaplains to be available in the Cathedral at all times. Yet he was never too busy or too tired to respond to those who needed him simply as a priest. The Cathedral has had many saints. Perhaps Julian Bickersteth was one of them. It shall be said in his honour that he would put aside all the deedy busy-ness of administering a diocese, for the sake of administering the Sacraments — if only to one sick old lady, who was regularly comforted by his visits and did, quite literally, listen for his footsteps.

The ashes of Julian Bickersteth were interred in the Chapel of St. Nicholas. The following words are inscribed on one of the stones of the pavement.

FOR THIS GOD IS OUR GOD
FOR EVER AND EVER
HE SHALL BE OUR GUIDE
EVEN OVER DEATH.

Beyond the Crypt transepts, to the east, are the two chapels of St. Gabriel and the Holy Innocents, corresponding to St. Anselm's and St. Andrew's in the upper part of the church. St. Gabriel's is a marvel of twelfth century frescoes, revealed to the public in 1952, when the roughly made wall which for centuries had blocked up the sanctuary was removed. The existence of these paintings was already well known. A number of experts, including Professor Tristram, had examined and treated them, in cramped and uncomfortable circumstances; before the common sense and initiative of Dean Hewlett Johnson, characteristically, let in the light.

Various reasons have been suggested for the walling-up of the apse. One is that the monks were intent upon hiding something precious, possibly even the coffin containing the body of St. Thomas. This could have happened at the time when the Community was preparing to go into exile during the reign of King John. John had a

'The Cathedral has had many saints' . . . The Chapel of St. Nicholas in Ernulf's Crypt, resting place of the ashes of Julian Bickersteth.

temper more violent even than that of his father King Henry II. The
contumaciousness of the brethren of Christ Church was too much
for him. He denounced them as traitors and obliged them to flee
precipitately for their lives. For six years the entire Community was
in exile in France; and it is natural to suppose that, before leaving,
they had taken steps to protect their more valuable treasures — not
to mention those invaluable bones — from the vengefulness of an
impious King. In doing so (if that is indeed the explanation) they
protected more than they knew. Since that time all the paintings
which covered the walls of the Crypt have vanished, with the exception of these few, as a result of limewashing or deliberate mutilation
or simply the wear and tear of exposure to the environment throughout centuries of indifference. It has to be admitted, however, that a
less romantic theory has now been more or less generally accepted
by historians and archeologists. This is to the effect that the entire
structure consisting of St. Anselm's Chapel and this one of St.

Gabriel's beneath, had to be shored up at a very early date as a result of a tendency to sink.

The painting above the central pillar on the chord of the apse represents a majestic Christ. The figure is surrounded by a mandorla (aureole) and supported by four angels. On either side of this group are six-winged angels standing on wheels. The south wall of the apse has a painting of the Annunciation to the Virgin, that on the north the Annunciation to Zacharias of the birth of St. John. Zacharias has been represented with no mouth to indicate that he was struck dumb in punishment for his disbelief. The soffit of the eastern arch is devoted to the Angels of the Seven Churches of the Apocalypse. All this wealth of painting has recently been very finely and expertly cleaned and restored. A programme lies ahead for the treatment of the main body of the chapel, where it is thought that much else remains to be revealed. The overall scheme is clearly intended to be a glorification of the Angelic Host. Angels these are indeed: fearful and wonderful, denizens of another world, remote from human life. We do not wonder that Mary was 'troubled' and afraid when she looked up from her prayers and beheld one of these.

THE CHAPEL of the Holy Innocents, on the north side of the Crypt, corresponds to that of St. Gabriel on the south. For those who come alone or in a small group, there is no better way of leaving the Cathedral than to enter this chapel last of all and linger in it, before going out by the north door into the ambulatory beneath what used to be the Prior's chapel — and proceeding to explore what remains of those buildings which used to be the domain of the monks.

This little chapel is dark and full of peace. If one turns on a light, two exceptionally beautiful romanesque pillars are revealed. The one in the centre of the chord of the sanctuary-apse, almost blocking out the view of the altar, is carved all over with what appear to be palm leaves, delicately veined and lying like the feathers of a bird or the scales of a fish. (In fact they are variously referred to in the guidebooks as leaves, feathers and scales.) Possibly, since the chapel is dedicated to the Holy Innocents, it was thought that so many small martyrs required an exceptional number of palms: the notion may seem peculiar to us, but would not have done so to the crafts-men who produced those leaves or to the monks who directed their work.

Within the apse on the south side of the altar, a memorial tablet

Palm leaves? feathers? fish scales? The romanesque pillar before the altar of the Holy Innocents. The design is believed to be unique.

has recently been inserted in the pavement. It is inscribed in memory of Gertrude Ferguson 'who for many years devoted her love of beauty in flowers to the adornment of this Cathedral and to God's greater glory'.

Mrs. Ferguson (few people, if anyone, at the Cathedral ever called her by her Christian name) 'did the flowers'. She did them as no one else had ever done them or will ever do them. An unwieldly barrel of a woman, she plodded up and down the aisles with her slopping buckets and her armfuls of frequently dripping greenery making a trail behind her as she went. Two great flowerpieces on pedestals at the east end of the Nave and two more in the Quire were the basis of her schemes. Another favourite spot was the niche

The capitals in the Holy Innocents Chapel are unlike any others in the Cathedral and show a strong Germanic influence.

Below
'Monkey Tree': a characteristic flowerpiece by Mrs. Gertrude Ferguson.

above the altar of Our Lady Undercroft before it was occupied by the ivory statuette: here she would put a few roses perhaps, deep red, with a tendril or two of something unexpected thrusting up at the back, always precisely and startlingly right. For Mrs. Ferguson was a genius with flowers. Not for her the standard arrangements of our post-war 'Flower Festivals' and Women's Institutes. Her masters — and masters they were; there was nothing suggestive of the feminine in her work — were those Dutch painters whose names one is inclined to forget, whose tumbling flowerpieces merge together in our minds: great green succulent leaves, poppy heads, overblown tulips, dewdrops, crawling insects, overturned nests. 'Fergy' refrained from introducing the nests. But she had an affection for cabbage leaves, especially of the crinkly variety, and for enormous bullrushes — and once she produced something called a Monkey Tree which looked like a living creature with swirling limbs. Long before any of us had heard of controlled scientific experiments to ascertain the psychic sensitivity of plants, Fergy would talk endlessly and with elaborate politeness to her flowers — and very impolitely indeed to such visitors as were rash enough to pause and attempt to watch her at her work. She disliked being asked questions and was apt to give peculiar replies; also she was apt to advance fiercely towards any female who came into the Cathedral with less on than she, Mrs. Ferguson, considered to be appropriate, and lay a substantial and accusing finger on the offending area of flesh. Throughout the war she worked on without assistance. Living alone in a small house in the Precincts, she was terrified (as were most of those who for one reason or another had chosen to remain) out of her wits by the bombs. She stayed because she loved two things above all: flowers and the Cathedral. The one she held to be worthy of the other. Her own art was worthy of both; and she must have known this, humble as she was.

THE ENTIRETY of the Crypt is associated with an extraordinary vision, gaudy and beautiful in a manner which recalls to us the 'great dreams' beloved of Dr. Carl Jung, with their scintillating archetypes. This vision or dream was experienced by one Master Feramin, physician to the monks. William of Canterbury, contemporary chronicler of the murder of Archbishop Thomas Becket, records two visions granted to this worthy citizen 'of honest conversation', the second of which he describes as follows:

'The same physician saw upon another time that he had come with certain others to go into the monastery of Canterbury. And lo, there was a man at the door clad in white raiment, holding a rod, who prevented him from entering, saying: *None shall enter in hither except he be crowned.* The physician stayed, making as if to go in but since it was not permitted him he said, *I will enter in by another way.* When he had betaken himself to another doorway, he found the same man standing there, just as before. When yet again he remained seeking entry for himself, the Keeper of the Door said unto him: *Stay here a little space,* and going away from the entry, returned from within bearing garments, with which he clothed those who stood waiting at the door, setting crowns upon their heads. Then he brought them even unto the High Altar, saying: *Kneel down and pray here.* This being done he turned again back through the Choir, through which he had come, going down into the Crypt, on that side where afterwards Thomas received the Crown of Martyrdom. And behold, throughout the length of the Crypt, from the entrance even to the uppermost part, there were to be seen seats in rows. A path for the newcomers lay between the rows, while there sat there Queens, crowned with diadems of gold, worked with precious stones, all marked with regal dignity and splendour, though each bent her head upon her hands, manifesting sorrow in her silence. Therefore the physician stopped as he came in, amazed by so much magnificence, wondering at the majesty and number of so many Queens, for indeed the multitude thereof exceeded all number. But their companion went on before, and passing through the midst of the Queens, came to the pillar where the body of the Holy Martyr from the time of his suffering lay buried for many years. Lifting up his eyes he saw there a Cross of Gold, of wondrous size, and a Man fixed thereon, while in astonishment he cried: *He is fairer in form*

Chapel of Our Lady Undercroft, seen from its north ambulatory.

than all the children of men. Now this was done that the Passion of Our Lord might be called into remembrance. Then Feramin was warned by his guide that he should bear record of his vision. When he had thrice spoken this into his ears he warned him yet again, lest he should leave it to be forgotten.'

Bᴇʏᴏɴᴅ ᴛʜᴇ Holy Innocents is the Eastern Crypt. Here behind the altar of the Undercroft, the body of St. Thomas was enshrined for the fifty years immediately following his death. (Not many years ago, when part of the flooring was removed for some practical purpose, a body was found which was thought to be that of the saint: had he never been 'translated' after all? — or had he been hidden by the monks from the trumpetings of King Henry VIII? Theories flew; until the poor remains were submitted to the cold scrutiny of 'experts', who pronounced them to be those of some person unknown and, save to his Maker, unimportant.)[1] Here, before the Trinity Chapel was begun, William the Englishman gave expression to his own genius, unhampered (one assumes) by the plans of his predecessor from France. The place is a kind of counterpoint of stolidity and grace. Immense round pillars support the vast weight which presses upon them from above, while slender marble columns spring upwards, spouting into a dancing display of cascading shafts: fountains or flowers; one is subtly reminded of both. 'And where', asks one visitor after another, 'is *Becket's ghost?'* (*Blessed Thomas the Martyr, give me patience.*) 'Over there, you see, on that pillar. Yes, it does look like a man, in a certain light. It was probably made by heaped up coal, when this part of the Crypt was used as a coal dump.'

For parties being shown round the Cathedral, Becket's ghost is usually the last item to be pointed out. After that:

'We'll go outside now and look at the Cloisters. Would you care to say a prayer before we leave the Cathedral? In the Undercroft perhaps, like the Black Prince.'

How many prayers, dignified and undignified, have been uttered with the lips and in the heart, in this cave-like place where 'the Virgin hath an habitation . . . somewhat dark'? *Ave Maria, Gratia Plena . . . Please God, let the All Clear go now, please, please God. . . .* So one more party gets up from its knees and goes out by the north door, passing by the Water Tower and proceeding through the vaulted tunnel which used to run beneath the Great Dortor where

[1] A fascinating account of this discovery is given in some letters written in 1888 by a Miss Holland, daughter of one of the Canons. The skull was received directly into the hands of the girl's mother. The letter-writer made a 'pall of thin white sarsnet silk with a broad edge of lace' to cover the bones while they were being kept in a room in the Precincts. Mr. Austin, the Cathedral surveyor, came out vehemently in support of the Becket theory; while Dr. Brigstocke Shepherd, Seneschal of the Cathedral, commented succintly: 'Piff paff.' 'But,' observes Miss Holland, 'he is evidently at daggers drawn with Austin.' Tragedy intrudes upon comedy as she goes on to relate how a blind child was brought to the Cathedral and directed by his father to press his own eyes against the eye-sockets of the 'saint'.

Overleaf
View from the NW corner
of the Cloisters showing on
the extreme right the
latest restoration in Lepine
stone, alongside all that
now remains of the work
undertaken by Prior
Chillenden. The two bays
on the left were restored
earlier this century.

Below
The Eastern Crypt built
circa 1180 by William the
Englishman. This was the
site of Becket's tomb until
the year 1220 when the
body was translated to the
Trinity Chapel above.

the brethren slept — to visit the place where they all of them used to pray and play and walk and work and sometimes, when the rule permitted it, even talk: four covered alleyways surrounding a square green garth.

The Cloisters were rebuilt in the late fourteenth and early fifteenth centuries under the auspices of Prior Chillenden, at the same time as the Nave. What remains of that rebuilding is disintegrating fast. It is easy, at a glance, to distinguish three periods: the ancient bays, the restoration carried out in the nineteen thirties and that which belongs to the period since the Second World War. Under the present scheme of restoration, little or nothing of the original work will be left visible from the garth. Meanwhile, as the operation progresses, extraordinary finds in the depths of the rubble above Chillenden's vaults, suggest that the pre-Chillenden Cloisters, built (it is believed) under Wibert, were by far the most lavish in England, decorated with fantastic carvings — some of which have been rescued and may eventually be exhibited or (better still) re-used within the Cathedral itself.

The Cloisters constitute the heart of what, for the monks, was 'home' in a domestic sense. Here, on the north side of the Cathedral, the Community pursued its daily life. The doors in the north alley led to the refectory, behind which lay the kitchens: a place, no doubt, of tremendous activity and importance. The east wall, north of the passage-way, is still in part that of the great Dormitory. This was rebuilt as the Library and received a direct hit during the war, from the bomb which fell nearest to the Cathedral itself. Since then, it has been again rebuilt; but the row of upper windows dating from the time of Lanfranc, is visible still above the Cloister roof.

The greater part of the monastic building was systematically destroyed in the reign of Edward VI. Little now remains apart from the Cloisters, the adjoining ambulatories which lead one past the Water Tower and out into the Green Court, and further to the east the ruins of the Infirmary, which survived as a result of being incorporated into various houses (since pulled down) which were built to accommodate the clergy of the new foundation. It takes an effort of the imagination, now, to visualise that teeming life of monks and servants. In the Green Court itself were the Prior's establishment (roughly on the site of the present Deanery); the breweries, granaries and stables (furthest north); and the two great halls which were used for the accommodation of guests. One of these stood in the south-west corner, adjoining the kitchens. This was for the middle-class guests, who no doubt insisted upon their meals being hot. The VIP's were in the house known as Meister Omers in the extreme north-east corner of the Precincts. Poorer pilgrims were housed in the Aula Nova or North Hall, of which the beautiful norman staircase still remains, in the north-west corner of the Green Court. The Infirmary Cloister extended along the east side of the little garden in front of Prior Wibert's Water Tower. Along the bottom of this garden, from the Dormitory to Prior Sellenges Gate, ran the Necessarium, which must have been a considerable affair and not particularly pleasant to have beneath the windows of one's sleeping quarters — although, doubtless, its position was convenient for peregrinations in the night; moreover, as a result of the activities of Prior Wibert, the drainage system was at least superior to anything which was likely to be found outside the convent. Prior Sellenges Gate is so called because it was built and used by that Prior, who had a study in it. Late fifteenth century in date, it is the way of approach to the Cathedral from the Green Court and a charming ornament: less so than it used to be, however, in the days before it was so meticulously cleaned up. Out here, among the various out-

buildings and monastic ruins surrounding the Cathedral, one wonders if some compromise could not be reached between those who are exclusively concerned for the health of the stonework and those who appreciate the beauty of an occasional tuft of flowers here and there and a trail of Russian vine or clematis. Not so many years ago a profusion of clematis used to tumble over Prior Sellenges Gate. In those days there were flowers growing out of the crumbling walls wherever one looked.

But if flowers and even ivy can be missed, pondweed, except perhaps in ponds, is less pleasing to look at. The monastic ruins may be neat as a new pin; but spreading all over the north walls of the Cathedral itself, a crop of green algae draws attention to the deplorable condition of those walls and the extent to which they have consistently suffered from neglect. Anyone who loves the building for its own sake must wonder at the indifference of successive generations of its custodians, who seem to have taken the view that what is not immediately seen is of little importance. The north side of the Cathedral is virtually hidden by the ambulatory which runs alongside it. Is it therefore to be relegated to the pigeons, the workmen (who set up their huts there and deposit all manner of junk) and the ravages of damp? For those who take the trouble to explore this region, it possesses a melancholy charm entirely peculiar to itself. A place of odd passageways and slypes, it offers no sweeping prospects of architectural magnificence, but sudden revelations of unexpected beauty in the straight lines of norman arcading, stained and rain-eroded, vanishing here and there into the dark recesses of some narrow slit between two walls where a transept or a chapel juts out. Here one can actually, even on a summer's afternoon at the peak of the season, be alone. One cannot help wondering whether some of the money at present being spent on cleaning the interior of the Cathedral (apparently on the principle that simply to look old is in some way indecent) could not be more happily employed in removing the slime and grime from these sunless walls and generally brightening the place up, in belated recognition of the fact that no part of the building is more worthy of our loving attention and respect.

In the east walk of the Cloister, not far from 'Becket's doorway' which leads into the Martyrdom, is the entrance to the Chapter House. This imposing room (one thinks of it as a room rather than a building because it is only from the inside that one ever really sees it) has an impressive fifteenth century wagon vault. The wall arcading is fourteenth century, reminding one of Prior Eastry's screens. The big windows are filled with typically Victorian glass. Here in the Chapter House the first performance of *Murder in the Cathedral* took place in 1935. This play was commissioned for the Friends' Festival of that year, on the initiative of Miss Margaret Babington. A year later, with equal perspicacity, she approached that great poet and theologian of the Church of England, Charles Williams, and asked him to write a second play for the Friends. The result was *Cranmer*

of Canterbury, a strange and haunting poetic drama of which a spectator wrote in the *Cathedral Chronicle* for July 1936:

> . . . the play was loosed. An hour and a half later the perfect voices of the singers declared 'world without end. Amen.' as though nothing had happened, and one rose unsteadily and went out. When thoughts had crept back to what had been a conventionally ordered mind before the hurricane, one remembered horrors and delights . . . the growing oppression of a trap closing in on Cranmer and on the mind . . . black gowned and masked Executioners with flames flicking in their hands; Cranmer running, stumbling into the arms of the Skeleton, the final appalling clarity, and then the cries, 'Speed! Speed!' and the rush of the flames down the aisle and Cranmer, pursued by the Skeleton, flying after them. . . . There was no appraising to be done, the play silenced both approval and censure into acknowledgement of greatness. The Spirits of Canterbury must have saluted it, well satisfied.

Writing of the 'new school' of Canterbury Cathedral drama, after this performance, the *Times*, in one of its more vapid and portentous moods, delivered itself of the following comment: 'If Mr. T. S. Eliot may be said to have founded it with *Murder in the Cathedral*, Mr. Charles Williams helps to establish its characteristics. This school of drama, written for performance in the Chapter House during a

Cathedral Festival, has no tradition to follow. The world has changed too much to allow the early, ecclesiastical Miracles — much less the later, civic Miracles — to stand for precedent; and religious plays written — by Mr. Masefield, Mr. Boulter and a few others — for performance in church have been too few to create a tradition. The Canterbury Cathedral drama could follow what course it would; and if it continues to be rather mystical than eventful, rather lyrical than dramatic, there is no reason why it should not develop on whatever lines it pleases.'

The *Times* did not know Miss Babington. She would have followed what course she would, without its permission. Unhappily, however, after those first two plays her judgement suffered a relapse. 'Canterbury Cathedral drama' sank into enjoyable mediocrity until the war put a temporary stop to it. It never completely recovered itself.

MARGARET BABINGTON died in 1958. A plaque commemorating her was inserted in the south wall of the Nave. Her ashes were interred in the Cloister garth. The plaque depicts a face of character, but with nothing of the witch-like individuality of the real woman. No one can ever have loved the Cathedral more or served it to better purpose than she did. She was indomitable. Twice she undertook an exhausting tour of the United States for the purpose of raising funds. The second time, she was approaching the age of eighty, crippled by illness and accident: still she succeeded in returning with the sum of £9,000. That is how money should be raised for the Cathedral: by love. She died at her desk in the Friends Office, working out plans for a third tour in the States. Of course she was difficult. Of course there were fantastic stories about her, some of them not entirely funny or pleasant. Towards the end it was said that she was too old to have entire responsibility for the running of the Friends; but the truth was that her value to the Cathedral was not to be measured in terms even of her practical work.

The Friends of Canterbury Cathedral was started by Dean Bell in the twenties; and Miss Babington was appointed as Steward and Treasurer by him. Between 1924 and 1963 Canterbury had three highly remarkable Deans. George Bell became Bishop of Chichester in 1929. When Temple died, it was generally expected that he would be the next Archbishop. Archbishops of Canterbury, however, are appointed by Prime Ministers: this was wartime, and Bell's views on the subject of the war had not always been acceptable to a belligerent government. He would not have cared greatly for such things; although he loved Canterbury and retired to the Precincts not long before his death. He was succeeded at the Deanery by 'Dick' Sheppard. 'Dick' came to Canterbury from St. Martin-in-the-Fields, the church he had so imbued with his own spirit of loving concern that it acquired a unique character, an all-embracing generous openness which attracts people to it, even now, at all hours of the day and night. After two years as Dean, the climate of the locality so affected his health that he was forced to resign. He died in 1937 and was buried in the Cloister garth. On the flat grave-stone are the words: THESE THINGS I COMMAND YOU THAT YE LOVE ONE ANOTHER. Dick's love was not only for 'humanity': it did not show itself only in his untiring and possibly over-simplistic work for peace; but in innumerable quirky little ways that were entirely peculiar to himself. In the nineteen twenties and thirties the Precincts was a tiny closed society in which one did not make friends on equal terms with 'the servants'. Dick chanced to discover that the Archbishop's butler played golf. The formidable Cosmo Gordon Lang was startled by a request from the Dean to challenge one of his servants on the links. He refused on the grounds that such unconventionality was indecorous and would not be understood. Dick repeated the request a second time with the same result. It was his prerogative as Dean to conduct the Archbishop in solemn procession to the Archiepiscopal throne whenever he attended a

Dean H.R.L. (Dick) Sheppard, outside the Deanery.

service. In the Martyrdom transept, on one such occasion, he paused.

'Cosmo', he murmured, looking round, 'may I play golf with the butler?'

'No, Dick, you *may not*.'

'In that case I am going to lead you into the Crypt.'

'Dick, this is outrageous. *Very well*.'

This story is given in Dean Hewlett Johnson's autobiography *Searching for Light*. Cosmo was extremely fond of both these 'rebel' Deans. But of Dick Sheppard it may be said that he was one of the very few people to pierce the armour of this lonely introverted man, who was so well known as the Archbishop, so little understood in himself. Dick could accomplish such miracles simply by his totally unselfconscious generosity and love. He assumed that he was Cosmo's friend – and so he became his friend. It would never have crossed his mind to wonder at his own achievement.

THE TWO gravestones lie side by side on the grass: Hugh Richard Lawrie Sheppard and Hewlett Johnson. The one was Dean for two years, the other for thirty-two. Hewlett Johnson was in office for longer than any other Dean; and of all those who ruled in Canterbury only old Henry de Eastry was there for longer still. The 'Red Dean' of Canterbury was famous – or notorious, whichever way you chose to put it – on account of his politics. The dramatic *charisma* of his personality added to the effect he created, acting upon his opponents as a positive irritant. What is not always realised is that Canterbury never had a better Dean nor one whose devotion to the Cathedral was put to greater tests. During the war, when many of those who were afterwards his most vituperative critics found reasons for leaving the city, the Dean stayed on. His wife and two young children were of necessity evacuated to Wales. (Hewlett Johnson was nearing seventy when his first child was born, of his second marriage: it must have been peculiarly hard for him to part from a family so lately acquired and so obviously dear to his heart.) The Deanery was bombed so severely that almost the entire facade of the house collapsed. Undeterred, the Dean accommodated himself in the one or two habitable rooms, happily issuing invitations to all and sundry who, for reasons connected with the war, were temporarily homeless: these invitations were gratefully accepted but not for any longer than was necessary, conditions being too spartan

Reunion after the enforced separation of war: Dean Hewlett Johnson with his wife Nowell, and daughters Kezia and Keren.

for most of his guests. Every Sunday evening he played classical records on his gramophone for the benefit of members of the Forces and anyone else who cared to come. For the few remaining residents of the Precincts the sight of that picturesque figure was an indescribable comfort. Charming, approachable and kind, he was always immaculately attired, always apparently unperturbed and optimistic. 'At least, Dean, you are properly dressed,' was the rueful comment of Archbishop Temple, when the Dean appeared at the Palace at three in the morning on the night of the June raid, every button of his black gaiters meticulously done up — surprising the poor Primate in his pyjamas no doubt.

Canterbury would have been a front line city in the event of an invasion of the Kentish coast. In 1940 such an event was expected almost hourly for months; and history has never altogether ex-

Dean Hewlett Johnson in old age. '. . . only old Henry de Eastry stayed for longer still'.

plained why it never took place. The Dean had been reliably informed that his name was on the list of those who would immediately be seized by the Gestapo and permitted to vanish without trace. The knowledge made no difference to his actions, and no apparent difference to his cheerfulness. He was doing, of course, no more than his duty as Dean. It would not have been necessary to emphasise these things – and he would have been the last person to wish to have them recalled – had it not been for the monotonous accusations that were levelled against him after the war by his political opponents.

Never at any time, before, during or after the war, did the Dean neglect his responsibilities to the Cathedral in the interests of politics. The time he spent in visits to China and the Soviet Union would never have been noticed had he used it to play golf or sail a boat. Certainly there were those among the truest and most loyal of his friends, who grieved over his political views and the actions arising out of those views. Such persons, however, were capable of 'seeing him whole'. They saw what he did for the Cathedral, and they saw what he was as a man. Unhappily, his colleagues on the Chapter were not amongst them. The odious, undignified exhibitions to which Canterbury was treated on the various occasions when the Chapter made an exceptional effort, in public, to get rid of their Dean, were scarcely an advertisement for Christian charity — except on the part of the Dean, who was unfailingly magnanimous. He was also, it must be said, remarkably obstinate. It was one of the paradoxes of his character that, while he was apparently incapable of bearing a grudge, he enjoyed a good battle; and one suspects that his continued occupancy of the Deanery until he was approaching the age of ninety, had as much to do with Canons and Archbishops as with anything else.

His gravestone bears these words:

GLORY TO GOD
PEACE ON EARTH
GOODWILL TOWARD MEN

He would have chosen that order of precedence.

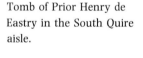

Tomb of Prior Henry de Eastry in the South Quire aisle.

THEY COME and they go, Archbishops, Priors, Deans, monks, vergers, choristers, lay-clerks: all of us pass through the story of the Cathedral and slide away with it into its past, wherever that goes — or stays — wherever it hides away in the stones, in the shadows, tantalising those who come after with intimations of its presence. And meanwhile there is one who goes on if not forever, at least for centuries. His name is *Argas Reflexus*. He is the Cathedral Bug.

Canterbury welcomes a new Dean. On 25th September 1976 Victor de Waal was installed as the latest in the long line of Deans of Canterbury.

Argas came (so it is said) back with the Crusaders from the Holy Land. In this, as in other things, he resembles the gnostic teachings associated with the Knights Templar and further back with the Islamic mystics. He is a very rare creature indeed; a species of tick. Nowhere else in England has he ever been seen. In these islands Canterbury Cathedral is his home; and it seems that he lingers here like the monster in Loch Ness, emerging occasionally and (possibly not liking what he finds) retreating once more into the dark and devious crannies where he leads his secret life. He is tiny and flat and hard, with a pear-shaped, tortoise-shell tinted back. When in motion, he is said to have eight legs. His longevity appears to be attributable to the fact that he can survive for a number of years without food. Nowadays, when people freely consume chips and other edibles in the Cathedral, one would suppose him to be entering upon a new and more hopeful phase of existence; however, he has not been seen for a long time; it may be that some new and deadly brand of aerosol has wiped him out. The last reported sighting was in the nineteen fifties, when the late Canon John Bouquet, in the act of consecrating the Host in St. Anselm's Chapel, perceived on the pure white linen altarcloth a motionless visitant. The Canon, being a knowledgeable old man, was in no doubt. It was Argas, come to assist at the celebration of the Eucharistic Sacrifice.

A GREAT DEAL has been said and written about the function of Cathedrals in the times to come. When the present Appeal Fund was launched, as a result of the discovery that millions of pounds would be needed simply to preserve the building in existence, the usual facile objections were put forward — by those who would not hesitate to spend money (as we all do) on personal luxuries and enjoyments — to the effect that we should not give financial aid to a building when human beings are in want. Human beings, however, can be starving in more ways than one. To live in close proximity to the Cathedral is to see for oneself how it draws people to it, how they come in their thousands, even millions, every year, in what would seem to be a confused groping after something, they scarcely know what, which they feel it has to give. The Cathedral is a centre of power. That power could radiate outwards, touching ordinary people, not necessarily Christians, not necessarily 'believers' of any sort, with a new understanding and a new hope.

We are passing, it seems, into a new age. Either we shall destroy ourselves by one means or another, or we shall discover fresh forms for man's universal need and desire to worship God, to adore the beautiful and to seek the Truth. Properly used and understood, the Cathedral could act as a spiritual power house for the furtherance of the work which must be done. It could be, for all those who enter it, a manifestation of the beauty of holiness. Certain elementary conditions, however, require to be fulfilled. If and in so far as the Cathedral is presented as a 'tourist attraction', it will be treated as such.

It has been said that the Cathedral needs money, therefore we must have 'audio-bars' and shops. The Cathedral needs nothing. When the world is no more worthy of such buildings, it will crumble away gently and return to the dimension from which it came and to which it properly belongs. Meanwhile it is we who need something. We need the Cathedral. But we need it as a place of holiness and peace. The money which is essential for its structural preservation will be found — when people understand it as a place which they need and must therefore support.

Cathedral in snow.

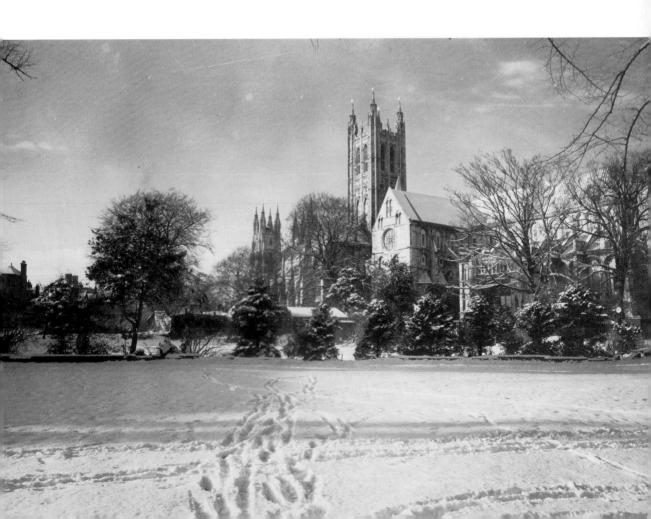

The problem of the din and disturbance created by vast crowds of people, many of whom appear to be treating the building as a picnic site rather than a church, is part of a vicious circle which, once it is understood as being such, will not be so difficult to break. The first and most obvious necessity is the total, relentless clearing away of 'audio-bars' and shops and everything else that is ugly and inappropriate. After that will come the more positive steps. Canterbury Cathedral is greatly loved. If, on the part of every single person who carries out responsibilities within its walls, there can be an impassioned caring, a tenderness of regard for the meaning underlying every stone and every pane of glass, that kind of miracle which is nothing but the working out of certain absolutely reliable spiritual laws – will simply come about. The ultimate goal must be found by a process of community experiment. I see it as the re-creation of a sacred place of which the main body of the church would be the holy sanctuary set apart for the performance of the rites; the Crypt would be a centre for the arts, for Religious Drama and Dance and, if they so desired, for the adherents of other Religions to come and enrich our tradition by their own rituals and prayers, sacred dances and songs. The side chapels would be used for groups practising meditation, spiritual healing and intercessory prayer. Meanwhile in the Precincts, such organisations as the Cyrenians, Shelter, Marriage Guidance, Child Welfare, Age Concern, Youth Groups of all kinds, would be encouraged to set up centres in organic connection with the church. A Guest House should be available for the renewal of the ancient tradition of hospitality, to be extended now towards all those young communities (such as Taizé and L'Arche in France, to name only two) whose experience could enrich and be enriched by our own. That is a remote ideal perhaps. But it need not be too difficult to make a start.

There have been many phases in the history of the Cathedral. In some, as during the last war, its spiritual reality has been drawn out; in others it has seemed to withdraw into the stones, waiting for the moment when once again it will meet with a response. The future will be as we choose. To permit oneself to get angry on behalf of so haughty and so humble a magnificence is of all things the most harmful and ridiculous. The Cathedral stands in its austere objectivity as far above our petty little angers as it is above those audio-bars and shops.

Let the Sufis have the last word:

Be with Me, not with thing. If anything reminds thee of Me, or concentrates thee upon Me, it only reminds thee of Me in order that thou mayest forget it, not Me, and that thou mayest be with Me, not with it; and it only concentrates thee upon Me in order that thou mayest be separated from it, not from Me.

IBN' ABDI'L-JABBAR AL-NAFFARI

Deans and Priors of Canterbury Cathedral

1845 William Rowe Lyall
1857 Henry Alford
1871 Robert Payne-Smith
1895 Frederick William
     Farrar
1903 Henry Wace
1924 George Bell
1929 Hugh Richard Lawrie
     Sheppard
1931 Hewlett Johnson
1963 Ian White-Thomson
1976 Victor de Waal

ARCHBISHOPS OF CANTERBURY

597 Augustine
604 Laurentius
619 Mellitus
624 Justus
627 Honorius
655 Deusdedit
668 Theodore
693 Berchtwald
731 Tatwin
735 Nothelm
741 Cuthbert
759 Bregwin
766 Jaenberht
793 Ethelhard
805 Wulfred
832 Feologild
833 Ceolnoth
870 Ethelred
890 Plegmund
914 Athelm
923 Wulfhelm
942 Odo
959 Alfsin
960 Dunstan
988 Ethelgar
990 Sigeric
995 Aelfric

1005 Alphege
1013 Living
1020 Ethelnoth
1038 Eadsige
1051 Robert
1052 Stigand
1070 Lanfranc
1093 Anselm
1114 Ralph D'Escures
1123 William de Corbeuil
1139 Theobald
1162 Thomas Becket
1174 Richard
1185 Baldwin
     Reginald Fitzjocelyn
     (*elected, but died*
     before consecration)
1193 Hubert Walter
1207 Stephen Langton
1229 Richard le Grand
1234 Edmund
1245 Boniface
1273 Robert Kilwardby
1279 John Peckham
1294 Robert Winchelsey
1313 Walter Reynolds
1328 Simon Mepham
1333 John Stratford
     John Ufford (*elected,*
     but died before
     consecration)
1349 Thomas Bradwardine
1349 Simon Islip
1366 Simon Langham
1368 William Whittlesey
1375 Simon Sudbury
1381 William Courtenay
1397 Thomas Arundel
1398 Roger Walden
     (*intruded*)
1399 Thomas Arundel
     (*restored*)

1414 Henry Chichele
1443 John Stafford
1452 John Kemp
1454 Thomas Bourchier
1486 John Morton
1501 Henry Dene
1503 William Warham
1533 Thomas Cranmer
1556 Reginald Pole
1559 Matthew Parker
1576 Edmund Grindal
1583 John Whitgift
1604 Richard Bancroft
1611 George Abbot
1633 William Laud
1660 William Juxon
1663 Gilbert Sheldon
1678 William Sancroft
1691 John Tillotson
1695 Thomas Tenison
1716 William Wake
1737 John Potter
1747 Thomas Herring
1757 Matthew Hutton
1758 Thomas Secker
1768 Frederick Cornwallis
1783 John Moore
1805 Charles Manners
     Sutton
1828 William Howley
1848 John Bird Sumner
1862 Charles Longley
1868 Archibald Campbell
     Tait
1883 Edward Benson
1897 Frederick Temple
1903 Randall Davidson
1928 Cosmo Gordon Lang
1942 William Temple
1945 Geoffrey Fisher
1961 Michael Ramsey
1974 Donald Coggan

Recommended reading

The following books are out of print but obtainable through libraries and (sometimes with difficulty) secondhand:

M. A. BABINGTON. *Canterbury Cathedral.* J. M. Dent. 1933.

BERNARD RACKHAM. *The Ancient Glass of Canterbury Cathedral.* Lund Humphries. 1959.
This huge unwieldy volume is a treasure to own. It contains illustrations of all the glass, many beautifully reproduced in colour, together with a comprehensive and scholarly commentary. It is, however, difficult and expensive to obtain. For ordinary purposes stick to the Ingram Hill pamphlet.

A. P. STANLEY. *Memorials of Canterbury.*
Generally known as 'Stanley's Memorials', this is a delightful old book, full of fascinating historical information. There have been various editions. Get whichever you can lay hands on.

S. A. WARNER. *Canterbury Cathedral.* SPCK. 1923.
This solid, well-illustrated guide book, light enough to carry round, is a 'must' for anyone making a serious study of the Cathedral. How you get hold of a copy is another matter.

WOODRUFF and DANKS. *Memorials of Canterbury Cathedral.* Chapman & Hall. 1912.
This comprehensive history of the Cathedral conveys so delightfully the character of its subject that it is worth combing the secondhand bookshops to find a copy. It is readable, entertaining and humorous. In addition it is a fat handsome volume, well-illustrated and well got up. Sadly, one has to admit that it is not always, from a scholarly point of view, entirely accurate.

The following books are presently available from all booksellers:

ST. ANSELM. *Prayers and Meditations.* Trans. and with an introduction by Sr. Benedicta Ward S.L.G. Penguin Books. 1973 (Paperback).
Invaluable as an aid to prayer and meditation, and for getting to know this holy and lovable saint.

JOHN BOYLE. *Portrait of Canterbury.* Robert Hale. 1974.
A good, downright history of the city (including, of course, the Cathedral) and discussion of its problems in the present, by one of its former Town Clerks.

LOUIS CHARPENTIER. *The Mysteries of Chartres Cathedral.* Trans. Ronald Fraser. Research into Lost Knowledge Organisation. 1972.
A clear, sane exposition of the mystical and esoteric aspects of Chartres Cathedral. Invaluable to anyone who wishes to understand Canterbury from a similar point of view. Paperback. Present price £1.50.

EADMER. *The Life of St. Anselm.* Ed. and trans. R. W. Southern. Clarendon Press. Oxford 1962.
Moving, amusing, readable. Translated into clear, fine, dignified modern English. A book in a million.

GARNIER's *Becket.* Trans. Janet Shirley. Phillimore. 1975.
A brilliant translation of the Life of St. Thomas in old French verse by Garnier de Pont-Sainte-Maxine, written between 1173–1175. Present price £6.50.

LAURENCE GOULDER. *Canterbury*. Pilgrimage Pamphlets. No. 1.
Obtainable from Guild Office, 2 Clement's Inn, London, W.C.2. Present price 15p.
An excellent and extremely useful guide to the Cathedral up to the time of the Reformation. Strong Roman Catholic bias.

DEREK INGRAM HILL. *Christ's Glorious Church*. SPCK. 1976.
A brief comprehensive history of the Cathedral by one of its Canons. Present price £1.95.

DEREK INGRAM HILL. *The Stained Glass of Canterbury Cathedral*. Published by the Friends of Canterbury Cathedral. Present price 18p. Essential guide to the glass.

HEWLETT JOHNSON. *Searching for Light*. Michael Joseph. 1968.
Autobiography of Dean Hewlett Johnson, justly described by Nowell Johnson as 'a testimony of his life-long search for truth and light'. Contains proof positive of his immense services to Canterbury Cathedral.

DAVID KNOWLES. *Thomas Becket*. Adam & Charles Black. 1970.
A scholarly and readable biography.

JOHN NEWMAN. *North East and East Kent*. 'Buildings of England' series. Ed. Nikolaus Pevsner. Penguin Books.
Contains an excellent architectural guide and commentary. Present price £3.75 (which for so small a volume is painful, but worth it).

OTTO VON SIMSON. *The Gothic Cathedral*. Bollingen Foundation. New York.
Essential for an understanding of the central idea behind the building of a medieval cathedral.

ROBERT WILLIS. *Architectural History of Some English Cathedrals. Part I*. Paul P. B. Minet. Chicheley. 1972.
This is Part I of a reprint in two parts of Professor Willis' papers on the architecture of some English Cathedrals, originally published between 1842 and 1863. For serious study it is invaluable. The book, which is beautifully illustrated and produced, costs £5 at the present time (1976).

Publisher's acknowledgements

The publishers are grateful to the following individuals and firms for the use of photographs:

Fisk-Moore Studios, Canterbury, pages i, 7, 11, 31, 33, 34, 35, 51, 61, 63, 69 87, 95, 102, 105, 111, 129 (bottom), 140 (bottom), 147, 150, 157

Janet and Colin Bord, pages 8, 12, 13, 19, 37, 38, 40, 44, 46, 47, 48, 49, 57 70, 71, 73, 76, 77, 83, 99, 113, 119, 120, 122, 123, 131, 132, 135, 136, 1 139, 140 (top), 141, 144/5, 155

Sonia Halliday and Laura Lushington, pages 7, 41 (and jacket: back), 70 (all from *Stained Glass* published by Mitchell Beazley); 6, 22, 23, 26, 27, 54, 55

Woodmansterne Publication Ltd., pages 15, 29, 45, 89, 98, 109, 114/115, 1. 143, endpaper, and jacket: front

Kent Messenger, pages 39, 47, 126, 127, 129 (top), 154

Charles Williams and Anne Spalding, page 149 (right)

Faber and Faber Ltd. and Angus McBean, page 149 (left)

Michael Holford, pages vi/vii

Alfred Deller, page 62

Royal Museum, Canterbury, and Entwhistle Photographic Services, pages ii/iii iv/v, 2, 10, 71, 79, 80, 85, 93, 107

The Dean and Chapter of Canterbury Cathedral, pages viii, 41, 102, 156

and to the following individuals and publishers for the use of quoted matter:

Mrs. Nowell Johnson for *Searching For Light* by Hewlett Johnson;

Faber and Faber Ltd. for *Murder in the Cathedral* by T. S. Eliot;

Paul P. B. Minet for *Architectural History of Some English Cathedrals* by Robert Willis;

Oxford University Press for *The Life of St Anselm* by Eadmer (trans. R. W. Southern);

Penguin Books Ltd. for *North East and East Kent* by John Newman;

Jonathan Cape Ltd. for *Kilvert's Diary* Ed. William Plomer;

The Research into Lost Knowledge Organisation for *The Mysteries of Chartres Cathedral* by Louis Charpentier;

The Dean and Chapter of Canterbury Cathedral for Prior Sellenge's letter to Archbishop Morton.

The publishers would also like to thank the Dean and Chapter for their co-operation in providing copyright permissions and for allowing photographs for this book to be taken inside the Cathedral.

Every effort has been made to trace copyright holders, and any omissions or errors brought to the publisher's notice will be corrected in future editions.

INDEX

The numbers in italics refer to illustration pages